Million
Dollar
Prospecting
Techniques

Other Books in The Million Dollar Round Table Series

Million Dollar Selling Techniques
Million Dollar Closing Techniques

Million Dollar Dollar
Prospecting Techniques

THE MILLION DOLLAR ROUND TABLE
CENTER FOR PRODUCTIVITY

JOHN WILEY & SONS, INC.

New York • Chichester • Weinheim • Brisbane • Singapore • Toronto

This book is printed on acid-free paper. ∞

Copyright © 1999 by The MDRT Center for Productivity. All rights reserved.

Published by John Wiley & Sons, Inc.

Published simultaneously in Canada.

This publication is designed to provide accurate and authoritative information in regard to the subject matter covered. It is sold with the understanding that the publisher is not engaged in rendering professional services. If professional advice or other expert assistance is required, the services of a competent professional person should be sought.

Designations used by companies to distinguish their products are often claimed as trademarks. In all instances where the author or publisher is aware of a claim, the product names appear in Initial Capital letters. Readers, however, should contact the appropriate companies for more complete information regarding trademarks and registration.

Library of Congress Cataloging-in-Publication Data:

Million dollar prospecting techniques / The Million Dollar Round Table
   Center for Productivity.
      p.   cm.
   Includes index.
   ISBN 0-471-32550-3 (pa. : alk. paper)
   1. Selling. 2. Selling—Insurance, Life. I. The Million Dollar
Round Table (Park Ridge, Ill.). Center for Productivity.
HF5438.25.M569   1999
368.32'0068'8—dc21   99-25931

Printed in the United States of America.

10 9 8 7 6 5 4 3 2

CONTENTS

INTRODUCTION

Prospecting is the labor of both successful and unsuccessful sales professionals. The difference between success and failure, however, is how the labor is performed. For some, prospecting is an arduous task that is filled with faded rainbows and empty pots of gold. For others, it is a glorious activity that is embraced with enthusiastic vigor and results in a high ceiling of success.

Ask top sales achievers how they approach prospecting. It's a sure bet their answers will be filled with confidence and certainty in their ability to sell their products and services. They will tell you that the fruits of their labor have produced bountiful results and that their success is directly related to their continuous prospecting endeavors.

The premise of this book is that you are already a sales professional, and now it's time to raise the bar. Why the title *Million Dollar Prospecting Techniques?* Simply because the core information you are about to read is directly culled from one of the world's most prestigious sales organizations—The Million Dollar Round Table. Before getting to the details of prospecting, let's address the question: What is The Million Dollar Round Table?

In 1927, thirty-two sales professionals who sold life insurance gathered in Memphis, Tennessee, to share sales ideas. They expected that the synergy of the group would enhance the professional skills of each participant. Today, the objectives of that group have grown into an international organization of nearly nineteen thousand members in forty countries, and have expanded throughout the financial services spectrum.

The Million Dollar Round Table commands universal respect. From a humble beginning, it has grown into the premier sales organization in the world. What is the MDRT magic? Over a long period of time, it has developed a set of core values, and these values have bound this prestigious organization together, nourished and sustained it, and made it the great organization that it is today. What better way to introduce this book and what the MDRT is all about than to articulate a number of these values and suggest how they can be used to help you realize your full professional and human potential.

MDRT's most important value is *productivity,* both on a professional and a human level. The Round Table was founded on a level of production that set the highest standard in the sales field, and today it represents the top 6 percent of sales representatives in the world. Within the organization, there are two additional levels of productivity, at three times and six times the basic entry requirements. The philosophy of this prestigious sales organization is "Dream big dreams" and turn those dreams into reality.

In 1962, Dr. Mortimer Adler introduced the concept of human productivity to MDRT. Dr. Adler challenged MDRT members to understand the intrinsic need of all human beings—particularly successful human beings—and to reach both inside and outside themselves so that meaningful lives can be achieved for more people. Essentially, what Dr. Adler presented was an idea whose time had come for The Million Dollar Round Table. Its members had reached a point where they realized that sales success is not enough; life is more than the sum total of what a person does for a living. Who an individual is is more important than what an individual does. Dr. Adler said that some aspects of life allow a person to simply live, and other aspects permit a person to live well. The Round Table adopted what it now calls the Whole Person Concept, a balance of seven vital life parts: (1) health, (2) family,

(3) spiritual, (4) education, (5) financial, (6) service, and (7) career. By definition, whole persons are engaged in a lifetime quest to achieve balance and congruity in all aspects of their lives and to continually seek the development of their full human potential.

Grant Taggart, a late Past President of MDRT, expressed the Whole Person Concept very well: "Personally, I believe in the acquisition of property and the making of money, but I contend such is not the all-important thing. Someone has said that, when you sum it all up, success isn't gold, it isn't in doing some deed that is bold. For the money we make or the houses we build mean nothing the moment one's voice has been stilled. But he or she has succeeded who, when he or she has gone, in the hearts of people is still living on." This philosophy has made MDRT sales professionals the successes they are today.

MDRT's *sharing and caring spirit* is a value that is cherished by its entire membership. Born at the original meeting in 1927, it has become a hallmark of the organization. MDRT has a rich tradition of sharing knowledge for the benefit of its members, its clients, and its members' companies. Unselfish concern for each other reflects MDRT members' truly unique and positive quality.

Commitment to excellence is a value that pervades the organization as well. Nowhere is this value more evident than at the Annual Meeting, considered to be the finest sales meeting in the world. The greatest tribute paid to this meeting is that many MDRT members spend more than 10 percent of their annual income to attend it. As evidence of MDRT's commitment to excellence, more than 1,200 members actively serve the organization each year, and MDRT's professional staff is a model for other sales organizations around the world. Superior performance has become MDRT's minimum standard.

In 1969, Marshall Wolper, an MDRT member, gave MDRT a new value by challenging each of his MDRT associates to *"Always stay over your head."* His basic premise: Don't be afraid to try a new market because you have limited knowledge. One doesn't learn how to sail by reading a book. Jump in and give it your very best; you will learn by doing, and you will grow by working diligently in your new selling endeavors.

Dr. Alec McKenzie gave the organization an important value with his *time management* philosophy, "No one has enough time, but everyone has all there is." Through McKenzie, MDRT associates learned about time wasters and the importance of delegating tasks to others. When sales professionals practice time management, their time can be spent on doing the job they do best— meeting prospects and clients to uncover and then solve their problems. MDRT sales professionals are, first and foremost, problem solvers.

A reinforced value for MDRT members is the importance of *goal setting*. The members need to know what they want from their business and their personal lives, and then set their sights on achieving those goals. Goal setting gives sales professionals a track to run on and the ability to measure their progress. MDRT members have learned that they can achieve what their minds can conceive. They dream "big dreams," and then set their goals to realize those dreams.

The Million Dollar Round Table has stressed the value of *professionalism*—conducting oneself as a professional in all activities. New members can learn or enhance their professional skills. MDRT sales professionals firmly believe that they must be good at who they are and what they do.

Although many other values could be mentioned, the final one that should be highlighted is MDRT's emphasis that its members should take the high road and demonstrate, by their leadership, that it is not enough to do what is legal or even what is ethical. They must always choose to do what is right. They firmly believe that one need never be contrite for doing the right thing, and taking the high road in all facets of life is the right thing to do.

What is the result of accepting the MDRT value system and Whole Person Concept? Quite simply, phenomenal sales and personal success, and this sales success is transferred to you throughout the chapters ahead.

Chapter 1

Prospecting Intangibles

S uccess in prospecting goes beyond having the right skills and applying the best systems. Although the right skills and the best systems are important requirements, it's the intangibles that serve as a catalyst to a successful sales career. A number of intangibles enter the success equation, the most important being:

✓ *Attitude*—How you feel about prospecting and sales.

✓ *Authenticity*—The conviction or belief you have in what you have to sell.

✓ *Defeating call reluctance*—Losing the fear of contacting the next prospect.

✓ *Applying your strengths*—Knowing what you are best at and using those skills to your advantage.

✓ *Overcoming the fear of rejection*—Losing the fear of hearing a "No" from the prospect.

Let's examine these intangibles and see how each of them works in unison to help you become an elite sales professional.

Attitude

When you achieve any kind of success in your sales profession, people want to know how you did it. This is certainly true in any business: everybody wants to know the secret to success. Book upon book has been written on the subject, and many success stories have been examined. Yet, there is no one exclusive secret. This should not prevent you from trying to acquire the ingredients needed to attain success, or from following the patterns of successful people.

Although much has been written and discussed about the factors that lead to success, most successful sales professionals can tell you face-to-face that all the successful people they know have one thing in common: They like what they are doing and certainly feel good about it. In other words, their *attitude* is positive, and they transmit that attitude while doing their jobs.

Those who want to succeed must pay the price and make a real and honest effort to do the fundamental things that have to be done. As the saying goes: Accept the things you cannot change, and change the things that can be changed. To succeed as a sales professional, you must find a way to sell, and the only way you can do this is by opening the door to a prospect's interest. Only then can you make a sincere effort to discover what your prospects need and incite them to act. This takes courage, perseverance, ambition, desire, and belief in oneself—all components to your best ally, your attitude.

How important is attitude? Many successful sales professionals will tell you that they can succeed without experience (some are successful from day one), without ability (they just have to work harder), and without knowledge (they sell simple solutions to simple needs). But they will also tell you that they cannot succeed without the right attitude, that is, a proper disposition toward what they do and how they communicate with people. As in any business, activity is the key to success, but not just any kind of activity. The only kind of activity that generates success is activity that places you in front of prospects and customers.

The right attitude plus activity is a guaranteed formula for success. Experience, knowledge, and a market are essential, but without the proper attitude, these attributes mean very little. It's a wonder that so few people accept this—not only in business, but in almost every facet of life.

Attitude is so powerful that when you are *sincere* and really want to take your prospect's best interest to heart, your actions and attitude will be reflected in his or her positive decision to buy. It's not the words you use that are most important; it's how you use them! Do your prospects understand? Are they convinced? Use simple language. Make it easy to understand. Keep it simple: they will have a hard enough time saying "Yes," so don't make it more difficult for them by making it hard to understand what you are selling.

Prospects don't want to buy fancy literature; they simply want to know what they will receive. What are the benefits of your products and services to them? Sales professionals sometimes forget that they are only paid when they succeed in making their prospects and clients act. When you don't succeed, your prospects may very well be at risk because they didn't accept the proposal you offered. The only reason prospects become customers is because the sales professional made them act, and once they become customers, they change. An overwhelming percentage of future sales will be made to your repeat customers. Is there any better proof of confidence?

Yes, the common denominators of success in sales are many: good training, continuing education, involvement in the industry you work in. Yet, the one that stands out as the most important determining factor of sales success is a *positive attitude*. It's imperative that you have a positive attitude about what you do.

Successful sales professionals have a positive opinion of what they sell and of how the general public views their business. A positive attitude may even be the primary reason successful sales professionals are consistent in their production and don't have the ups and downs that plague less successful sales peers.

MDRT members identify enthusiasm and self-confidence as two of the most important contributors to their success. Asked about a time when they were particularly productive, sales professionals—high and low performers alike—invariably say that one of the reasons they were particularly successful during that time was because they had a positive attitude.

You may believe that you already have a positive attitude; indeed, your positive attitude might be one of the primary your manager hired you into the business. Still, for even the most positive-minded people, it's hard to be "up" all of the time. Life is not always easy or fair; after all, it is human to be overcome at times by negative thoughts or events.

Successful, productive, positive-minded sales professionals not only realize this, but also realize that, regardless of one's personal feelings or circumstances, a positive attitude is helpful—even necessary—in selling one's products and services.

With this in mind, successful sales professionals conscientiously take steps to ensure that their attitudes remain positive. What can you do to develop and nurture a positive attitude? First, purposefully adopt a positive attitude. We all know that attitude is a state of mind. This being the case, it is surprising that many people, without even realizing it, decide to take on a negative rather than a positive attitude. Given the choice—and people are given this option—why not decide to be positive? Like the pebble thrown into the pond, the ripple effect of your attitude is bound to have an impact on the people around you: your friends and family, your coworkers, and your clients and prospects will be influenced by your attitude, be it positive or negative.

Authenticity

Many successful salespeople believe that it's also their attitude toward their profession, their products, and their company that influences their sales success. In fact, it's this attitude toward what they do that influences their prospects' attitudes toward them. They truly believe that this makes a world of difference when it comes to successful prospecting.

It's very hard to convince a person to buy a product if you don't believe in the product yourself. Your attitude toward your products and services should be quite simple: "The products I sell and the services I offer are second to none. I know I sell a product that has proven itself over time. The product has always done what it has promised to do. In brief, I sell one of the highest quality products a sales professional can market." Strong commitment, but necessary to succeed.

To sell a product, you must be convinced of its value and able to convince others accordingly. To convince them, you must gain your clients' confidence that you are acting in their best interest. This is best accomplished through a positive attitude about the virtues of your products and their benefit to clients and prospects.

How do you feel about the products and services you offer?

It isn't coincidental that the greatest sales professionals have an almost missionary zeal about their work and the service they provide. With such strong beliefs, these individuals are able to sustain a motivation level that is combined with a tremendous desire to produce more business than the "less convinced" sales professionals.

In many instances, your prospects will buy not because *they* are convinced, but because *you* are convinced. But if your prospects buy your belief, they will also buy your doubt. Therefore, to sell effectively, you must believe totally in the products and services you provide.

What if you don't feel zealous in your selling endeavors? The good news is that belief, like many other things, is rarely discovered—it is developed. To develop belief, though, requires focusing attention on it, and the one way to do this is to act in a manner consistent with your own beliefs. Remember: To believe is to regard something as true. In this context, you must believe that the actions you suggest to your prospects are truly beneficial to each of them and to their families. If you believe this to be true, then you are convinced; thus, your actions will carry conviction—the stamp of truth. If your actions do not carry conviction, then in most cases, your prospects will eventually shut you out. "He that complies against his will is of his own opinions still." You must be 100 percent convinced that the course of action you suggest is in your prospects' best interest before you can ever convince them of that fact.

One MDRT sales professional developed a simple system based on his belief in the products and services he sold. This exercise works if he is convinced of a prospect's need before he approaches the prospect. He calls this system Take Five, Get Five. It takes a few minutes to complete and is based on five key points in each of the following four areas:

1. *Prospect's needs:* Here you list five needs that you are convinced prospects have. The purpose is to have a clear picture of what prospects' real needs and problems are, and how your products and services match those needs.

2. *Reasons why:* Here you list five reasons why prospects should buy your products and services. To do this successfully requires empathy: there must be an understanding of the prospect's perspective. The stronger the reasons why the prospect should buy, the greater the level of conviction. If you can't think of any reasons why prospects should buy, then there's no reason for you to sell to them in the first place!

3. *Probable objections:* Here you list five reasons your prospects might give for not buying your products or services. Always include the obvious.

4. *Answers to objections:* Here you create five answers to each objection. Your answers to objections should be based on prospects' reasons to buy. The realization that

your prospects have a genuine need for your products and services will set you on your way. Then remind yourself that any objections prospects might raise will always be outweighed by the reasons they should go ahead with the purchase.

People generally have confidence in things with which they are familiar. They will accept and act on an idea when they can clearly understand how it will fit into their daily lives and help them. They will buy merchandise when they realize and can visualize a need for it and for what it will do for them.

On the other hand, almost everyone is suspicious of vague ideas, complex mechanisms, and half-explained facts. There is a strong tendency to reject altogether the vague, the complicated, and the hard to understand.

To sell anything, therefore, you have to be able to give a prospect a clear-cut, definite picture of just what it is and how it will meet his or her needs and wants. And, naturally, before you can do that, you have to have the clear-cut picture in your mind.

So, although "Know your product" may sound like a trite slogan in the it-goes-without-saying class, it's a basic bit of advice that can't be skipped over in any book on prospecting.

Moreover, as a sales professional, knowing your products should go a lot deeper than the simple phrase implies. That is, you must not only know all about what you are selling—how it's put together, how it works—but, more important, you must know how your product will benefit your prospect's way of life or plans for the future. You seldom make a sale by saying, "I think you'll like it." You have to explain why.

It is with this in mind that many, in fact nearly all, large organizations provide indoctrination courses for sales professionals before they ever send them on their way. A new sales professional may be given a step-by-step education in all the processes and raw materials that go into making the finished product he or she will someday be discussing with possible buyers. In addition, the new sales professional may even get the opportunity to shadow a coworker who has achieved high success in sales.

This all adds up to background knowledge. Very possibly, sales professionals will make little specific use of the data drilled into them when the activity of prospecting and selling actually occurs. Just as you seldom go around reciting the multiplication table you learned in school, you will rarely have to mention to a prospect all the various facts you have absorbed. But the fact that you know them will come across in your conviction and belief in your products and services. Your knowledge will give you confidence and the easy assurance that comes with being able to handle any questions or doubtful points that may arise; it will enable you to convince a prospect that you really know what you are talking about.

Of course, if you are in a business of your own, instead of being a member of a sales team in an established company, you have to do your own digging of facts about the products and services you sell. This may require a good bit of research, perhaps even extra schooling, if available. But you can be sure that whatever you have to do to pile up background and acquaint yourself with your subject matter is necessary and will pay off. It stands to reason that knowledge always pays off, even if only in the satisfaction that comes with having it.

Attitude, by definition, is a disposition. It reveals your inclination and nature. Your attitude shows prospects what you will do for them and also what your real intentions are. Why do people who are almost rude to you when you first meet them—giving you all sorts of objections—become your best customers, or, at times, become your friends, confiding in you on matters that they will not tell their friends or even their attorneys? Could it be that they recognize your conviction in the products and services you sell, your belief that what you do and sell can enhance your prospect's life in some way?

It is so important to realize that prospects don't really mean "no" when you contact them. They don't really mean it when they give the impression that you are an intruder, a solicitor, or a beggar! What they mean is "No, I'm not ready to buy. I have other priorities. I don't want to make these decisions. Besides, I don't know you, so why should I trust you?" It is of utmost importance that you understand that what they mean to say is "Convince me, don't give up! Are you for real? Do you really believe in what you do? Do you really want to help me?" These are the real concerns behind their apparent indifference.

It is not only essential that you understand this principle, but it is equally important that trainers and managers prepare salespeople for this reality of the job. Once you acknowledge and understand this, it makes a tremendous difference in your attitude. Successful sales professionals understand the fact that sales resistance (objections, hesitation, fear) is only natural. You should be thankful for this resistance, because without it, there would be little need for your services; people would easily recognize their needs and understand your products. Sales resistance makes your job vital, and this is the reason successful salespeople are well paid and able to enjoy the lifestyles they desire.

When you don't succeed in selling your products or services, chances are your prospects won't even remember your name. When you do convince prospects to make a decision to buy, they will—in some instances—remember you for the rest of their lives. Bear in mind that you are only as convincing as you are convinced yourself!

Therefore, it is very important to be prepared and to realize that prospects will object, not only to the sale, but to the interview itself. The better prepared you are, the easier it will be to open the door. Failure to do so results in a negative sales formula: No interview equals no presentation equals no sale!

It all begins with a "no." After a few years in sales, you will know all too well that most of the sales you made started not with a single "no," but with many "noes." One of the standing jokes among sales people is that if you ask a hundred people whether they want to buy your product or services today, 90 percent will answer "No"; the other 10 percent will answer "Hell, no."

To illustrate this point, let's visit a situation that occurred very early in the sales career of an MDRT associate, about thirty years ago. It has had a marked influence on him for many years:

> I had asked to meet the brother and partner of one of my clients. My client was the president of the firm, and I had sold him a substantial financial plan. After some hesitation, he introduced me to his brother with the following words: "Meet (my name)—and you had better watch yourself!" After his statement of introduction, the brother and I shook hands and my client left.
>
> Before I could say one word, the brother said, "I have heard of you, and I may as well tell you a few things right now. First, I have all the financial planning I need. Second, my financial planning program has recently been revised. Third, I have at least ten personal friends who are in the same business as you. And last, you could not have picked a worse time to come in, as this is our busiest time of the year. In fact, we are so busy we don't even have time to look after our own families."
>
> No doubt, this approach was one that he had used successfully with other financial planners. Had my feelings toward prospects' and clients' attitudes not been what they are, his objections would probably have sent me on my way. The easy exit would have been to leave my business card and suggest he contact me should he have need of my services.
>
> But that is not what I did. Instead, I said to him, "If you had told me you needed financial planning assistance, I would have been very surprised." I agreed with him that a program can always be revised and updated. I also agreed with him that, as a successful businessman, he was surely a

prime target for financial planners and that he probably knew ten or twenty of them who were in the business.

I acknowledged the fact that his time constraints obviously limited his precious family time. In short, he was an extremely busy man who had difficulty taking time for lunch and probably ate on the run sometime between noon and three in the afternoon.

He seemed pleased that I appreciated his situation. ("At last," he thought, "a financial planner who understands!") This feeling was somewhat reinforced when I informed him that I had been in his line of business before becoming a sales professional. At this point I said, "The only reason for my visit today is to meet you. I will return tomorrow at five minutes to noon, and if it so happens that you have a chance to eat between noon and three o'clock, I would like to take you to lunch."

I don't think he had heard this approach before. He hesitated for a few seconds and finally said, "Well, I certainly can't stop you from waiting." And before he could add anything else, I said thank you, shook hands, and left.

The following day at five minutes before noon, I knocked on his door. Do you think I waited the whole afternoon? Not a chance. About twenty minutes later, we went to lunch, and I sold him a large financial policy at the restaurant. He since then has become my best and largest client, and also developed into my best center of influence. Additionally, over the years, we have become close friends.

Why did this happen? It's pretty obvious: this sales professional understood his prospect's attitude. What does it really mean when the prospect objects to seeing you? In the example just presented, if the sales professional had heeded the prospect's initial objection, very likely a purchase would never have been made.

As a sales professional, provoking action is often your job. Have you wondered why it is that after the initial barrier is broken, prospects' attitudes toward you change so markedly? They confide in you and consult openly with you, and not only on matters concerning the products and services you sell. You become somebody they want to talk to, and they tell you things they won't tell others.

This shift in attitude is a part of the game of life: people want to do so many things and yet do so few. The relationship between a sales professional and a client develops as clients appreciate you for having had the know-how, the ability, and the conviction to help them do the things they wanted to do, sometimes for a long time. You've given them peace of mind—all because you care about what you do and it shows.

Defeating Call Reluctance

A common prospecting problem for a typical sales professional is the fear of making cold calls. There are many reasons for call reluctance, as you will soon see, and it can present itself in many ways. Think for a minute. Do you have a fear of using a telephone? You have probably experienced this sometime in your sales career. Or how about the fear of prospecting with friends and relatives? You feel that you want to do a good job for them, but it's uncomfortable for you to approach them. How about the fear of prospecting socially? You don't like the reputation of the person who corners someone at a party. How about the greatest fear of all, the fear of rejection? Actually, each of these other fears in some way relates to rejection, and you've probably experienced them all.

Let's examine the psychological aspect of call reluctance, which behavioral scientists have studied for many years. George W. Dudley, a pioneer in the field of behavioral studies, determined that there were nine psychological barriers that cause sales professionals to exhibit call reluctance.

Threat Sensitivity

This type of call reluctance occurs when the sales professional becomes preoccupied with worst-case prospecting possibilities. The threat-sensitive type of salesperson copes by staying alarmed and maintaining a high degree of emergency preparedness. This level of heightened vigilance is an emotional and physical drain on energy. It results in insufficient stamina for initiating contact with prospects on a regular basis.

Ask yourself, "Do I see prospecting in terms of social or emotional risk-taking? Do I rely on memorized sales scripts? Do I stay away from social involvement in civic, fraternal, or religious organizations?" If you have answered yes to any of these questions, you may be exhibiting a threat-sensitivity call-reluctance behavior.

Desurgency

Desurgent call reluctance occurs in sensitive sales professionals who become anxious about being swept away by the intensity of their own feelings. To cope, the desurgent person goes emotionally underground, developing interests in highly technical or artistic matters. He or she controls feelings by keeping them locked up and out of sight. Interaction with others is conducted through emotionally safe, information-bound channels: letters, e-mail, and so on. More time is spent preparing the information than actually prospecting.

Ask yourself, "Do I tend to censor myself from expressing what I really feel when I talk to prospects? Do I tend to lack enthusiasm in my business interactions? Do I think that public displays of emotion are signs of character weaknesses or insincerity?" If you have answered yes to any of these questions, you may be exhibiting a desurgency call-reluctance behavior.

Protension

Protension call reluctance occurs in sales professionals who try to compensate for suspicions they hold about their own personal value by overinvesting in the appearance and mannerisms of worth, accomplishment, and ability. The protension type of sales-person gets distracted from prospecting by becoming preoccupied with self-image and displaying symbols of success. Prospecting becomes a hustling activity that is demeaning and undignified. The result is a shallow or nonexistent client base.

Ask yourself, "Do I tend to react defensively whenever someone doubts my competency or integrity? Do I feel my appearance is the determining factor in my sales success? Do I seek alternative 'professional' means of prospecting in lieu of proven prospecting methods?" If you have answered yes to any of these questions, you may be exhibiting a protension call-reluctance behavior.

Groups

Fear of speaking before a group is a facet of call reluctance that occurs in sales professionals who are overanxious about appearance, approval, and acceptance. This type of sales professional becomes comfortable self-promoting in one-on-one situations but becomes distressed in front of groups. In a prospecting scenario where seminar selling or work-site marketing selling is emphasized, this type of call reluctance can be catastrophic.

Ask yourself, "Do I actively avoid opportunities to go before groups of various sizes to promote my products and services? Do I tend to be self-critical when I hear myself on tape or see myself on video? Do I tend to think that every speech I hear is better than anything I could deliver in person?" If you have answered yes to any of these questions, you may be exhibiting a groups call-reluctance behavior.

Friends

Friends call reluctance occurs when sales professionals become too protective about the way friends might react if the professional were to make a sales call on them or ask for a referral. They believe that their friends would be offended and feel exploited if they made a sales presentation to them. To avoid the loss of approval and protect their friendship, making a sales call is out of the question. Unfortunately, the competition does not recognize these emotional boundaries, and so a sales opportunity is lost.

Ask yourself, "Do I keep my friends and business interests absolutely separate? Do I purposelessly de-emphasize prospecting when I talk to friends about my job? Do I protect friends from managers and other salespeople in my organization?" If you have answered yes to any of these questions, you may be exhibiting a friends call-reluctance behavior.

Role Acceptance

Role-acceptance call reluctance occurs when sales professionals believe they ought to be in a career other than sales. Often, they believe they are a disappointment to some significant person in their lives, which results in shame or guilt. This puts a damper on expressing any energy or enthusiasm when approaching prospects.

Ask yourself, "Do I tend to be self-depreciating when I talk to other people about my sales career? Do I try to act positive in a contrived way around other salespeople? Do I try to find verbal replacements for the terms *salesperson* or *sales professional?*" If you have answered yes to any of these questions, you may be exhibiting a role-acceptance call-reluctance behavior.

Disruptive Sensitivity

Disruptive-sensitivity call reluctance occurs in sales profession-als who have difficulty asserting themselves, particularly when it comes to prospecting. Unwilling to risk being considered pushy, forward, or intrusive, they continually yield to the needs and interests of other people. In doing so, they put themselves on perpetual hold. Because prospecting is essentially an act of initi-ating contacts, these salespeople have trouble doing it. They are afraid that the prospective contacts might be busy or otherwise engaged. So they sacrifice sales opportunities by waiting for the "right" time or circumstances. These conditions are rarely met.

Ask yourself, "Do I often let people take advantage of me? Is talking to a prospect using a telephone easier than face-to-face prospecting? Is it difficult for me to handle a prospect who thinks I'm being pushy?" If you have answered yes to any of these questions, you may be exhibiting a disruptive-sensitivity call-reluctance behavior.

Social Differential

Social differential is a highly targeted form of call reluctance. Salespeople who have it can usually initiate contact with anyone unless that person is a member of a group they have selected to avoid for any number of reasons. It occurs in salespeople who are too socially self-conscious. They labor under a rigid, self-imposed psychological caste system that elevates people who have educa-tion, a position of authority, or wealth to levels of superiority that the salesperson emotionally considers out of his or her reach. They cope by simply avoiding contact.

Ask yourself, "Do I tend to be more childlike in the presence of certain people? Do I know a lot of professional people whom I should contact but haven't? Do I get secretly angry with myself for being so easy to intimidate?" If you have answered yes to any of these questions, you may be exhibiting a social-differential call-reluctance behavior.

Family/Relatives

Family/relative call reluctance occurs in sales professionals who are not emotionally emancipated from their parents. Adult in other aspects, they tend to regress to perceptions, emotions, and behaviors they knew as a child when they are around parents and relatives. They believe that trying to prospect among members of their own family would never work, for it would involve risking parental rejection and disapproval.

Ask yourself, "Do I ever feel the need to protect my family members from my manager or other salespeople in my organization? Do my family members know that I have been insulating them by not attempting to sell to them? Would I hesitate to give family members the name of a sales associate even if they requested it?" If you have answered yes to any of these questions, you may be exhibiting a family call-reluctance behavior.

You can turn any of these nine negative fears into something very positive for yourself. But it takes motivation and a willingness to improve. There's an old saying: "What you say to yourself about prospecting has a powerful impact on what you feel when prospecting. What you feel when prospecting has a powerful impact on what you do about prospecting."

Many successful sales professionals have turned rejection into their best prospecting tool.

First, let's define rejection with a true story: Tom Brown, from St. Paul, has been a very successful salesperson. As a matter of fact, in Tom's first year in the business with his company, he was one of their top salespeople. In his second year, he was the company's top second-year salesperson. In those first two years, Tom closed over two hundred sales opportunities. But after two years of success, Tom went to his boss and told him he was considering leaving the business. This didn't make any sense, so the boss decided that he should analyze what Tom was doing to see why he felt that way. Tom had had sales experience. He knew how to make cold calls. He knew how to prospect and he knew how to set goals. And Tom set a goal to call on ten people per week. Over those first two years, Tom called on over one thousand prospects, of whom Tom saw three hundred. Out of those three hundred prospects, Tom sold products to two hundred. By all standards, that's excellent production in your first two years. Yet, stop and think about it for a minute. In that short, two-year period of time, Tom was rejected over eight hundred times. Now that, truly, is rejection. This is the type of rejection that sales professionals, unlike any other professionals, experience regularly.

In a broader sense, why are so many people afraid to try new ideas, new ventures, or unusual approaches to solving problems? Because they are afraid to fail. Fear of failure is a human trait. Nobody wants to suffer the pains of defeat. But no endeavor can succeed unless it attempted, and with every attempt, there is the risk that it will not work.

In prospecting, as in many life events, you will fail often in your attempts to persuade a prospect to see the benefits of your products and services. Yet, you will learn from these rejections and learn to overcome them. The first time you try something new in a prospecting approach, there is a fair chance that you will not succeed.

Think about the first time you tried to put together a jigsaw puzzle and you almost gave up in frustration. The parts simply would not fit together. But with patience and determination, you began to identify patterns, and in a short while you turned a failure into a success. This happens with prospecting, too.

Even when you have experience and know-how, you cannot always be successful. There will be times when prospects continually reject you, but you must not let the concept of failure overwhelm you. R.H. Macy had to close his first seven stores, but instead of giving up as a failure, he kept trying and became one of America's leading retailers. Babe Ruth struck out over 1,300 times in his career, but that is forgotten because of his 714 home runs. Thomas Edison overcame rejection, as well. He never gave up, yet for him, perseverance was not enough. Each time one of his experiments failed, he studied what caused the failure and kept seeking solutions. He failed almost a thousand times before developing the filament that made the lightbulb work. Imagine being rejected a thousand times by prospects. It sometimes takes that one thousand and first attempt to turn things around.

When approaching prospects, you must psyche yourself to succeed. Expect rejections and project victories. They will come—it's all about attitude and how you view failure.

Applying Your Strengths

It's impossible to expect that you can do everything effectively in prospecting. That's why it's important to identify your strengths and weaknesses; determine what you are good at and use those skills to your advantage. One measurable way to identify your strengths and weaknesses is to determine your personality type. By doing so, you understand not only your style of selling but, more important, your prospects' style of buying.

The practice of identifying or measuring personality types or styles is known as psychometrics or behavioral analysis. This is a thriving business in North America and many other parts of the world. Today, it is a management science; however, its origins can be traced back more than two thousand years.

Let's examine a brief overview of personality types so that you can identify your own and determine how to sell to each of your prospects. For starters, there are four distinct personality types that are evenly spread throughout any given population: analytical, driver, amiable, and expressive. Being different, each of these personality styles has its own selling style, and each likes to be sold to in a particular fashion.

As a sales professional, you operate from one quarter of a four-quarter personality grid and relate best, from a business point of view, with others from the same group. This means that in your dealings with the remaining 75 percent of the population, you will be an opposing personality style, unless—and this is a big unless—you can adapt. One of the important characteristics of successful sales professionals is their ability to adapt their personality and approach to suit that of their prospect.

Now, you may feel that people cannot be easily pigeonholed into four well-defined groups. In a way, you are right; there aren't four distinct styles of personality, but many. However, over the years, extensive research by leading universities and thinkers shows that everyone has personality traits emanating primarily from one of the four styles.

It is likely that, in examining the four personality types, you will categorize yourself before you apply the process to your prospects. If you can position yourself, you can position others. However, no one personality style is likely to be more successful in sales than another style; instead, there are just different types of successful sales professionals! This is an important point because it is often perceived (by those with little knowledge on the subject) that there are "success types." This is not the case. All types have both positive (strengths) and negative (weaknesses) characteristics; no one group has a monopoly on positivity and enthusiasm.

The reality is that it's not what you've got, but what you do with what you've got!

Analytical Personality

The analytical personality describes a precise and systematic person who tends to follow set procedures in both business and personal life. This person not only likes things to proceed in an orderly manner, but also pays attention to details and is a conscientious worker. This person also likes to get all the details before making a decision. Being a highly cautious decision maker who is unlikely to depart from set procedures, the analytical personality type likes to work in a disciplined environment with operational guidelines. Usually, he or she is tactful and diplomatic and will not knowingly antagonize others. This individual will also avoid situations where conflict is likely. Often described as a "technical personality," this type of person is likely to ask a lot of detailed questions.

Adjectives that identify the analytical personality are disciplined, compliant, careful, systematic, accurate, logical, reserved, suspicious, self-conscious, and serious.

Typical questions asked by the analytical personality style are:

How long has your company been in business?

What guarantees can you give me about your products and services?

What assurance do I have that you will do the things you say you will?

How many customers have bought these products and services?

Driver Personality

Being direct and forceful, the driver personality type prefers a competitive environment and works toward the attainment of goals. This is a restless person who seeks new challenges and is often unconventional and creative in his or her problem solving. This person also sets high standards and is critical when others do not attain them, and is easily bored or irritated by routine tasks. This personality type resists being part of a team, preferring instead to find self-tailored solutions or answers to problems. This person can work without supervision or control and prefers to. He or she is blunt or overbearing with others and can be impatient. Often called a director or a control personality, this type of person has no time for formalities. Suffice it to say, he or she likes to get to the point quickly.

Adjectives that identify the driver personality are driving, competitive, forceful, inquisitive, self-starting, assertive, restless, impulsive, impatient, and demonstrative.

Typical questions asked by a driver personality type are:

What will it cost me?

Why should I buy from you?

What would happen if . . . ?

What makes this product better than a similar product?

Amiable Personality

The amiable personality describes an easygoing person who plans his or her work carefully and then works at a steady pace. This type of individual likes to get into a steady routine, does not adapt well to change, and is often content with things the way they are. The amiable person is reliable and will perform consistently, if not startlingly. He or she also prefers to work under instruction rather than use personal initiative. This type of person is indirect in dealing with others, unpretentious and undemanding, and usually gets along with people. Friendships are valued highly, and family ties are strong. The amiable personality type is often described as the relater personality because he or she is relationship-oriented.

Adjectives that identify the amiable personality are dependable, deliberate, easygoing, good listener, hesitant, undemanding, peaceful, conservative, and overcautious.

Typical questions asked by the amiable personality type are:

There is no rush to decide, is there?

How long have you been doing this job?

Can I take same information home and think about it?

You can guarantee its benefits, can't you?

Expressive Personality

A person with an expressive personality is someone who is gregarious, makes friends easily with strangers, and is socially adept. This person places great importance on relationships with others (often at the expense of results), enjoys public recognition, and seeks social acceptance. Willing to help others, the expressive personality type can show great enthusiasm for the ideas of others as well as for his own or her own. Preferring to do business on a social basis, this type of person has an extensive network of friends. This individual often has difficulty planning his or her time and judging the abilities of others. Described as the socializer personality, the expressive personality type is recognized by a friendly, outgoing manner.

Adjectives that identify the expressive personality are charismatic, influential, affable, verbal, persuasive, impetuous, active, energetic, restless, and impulsive.

Typical questions asked by the expressive personality type are:

Can we meet and discuss this over lunch?

Can I bring a friend along so you can explain this to both of us?

It seems all right, but can you explain that part again?

I'd like to show this to my friend before I decide. That's okay, isn't it?

Now that an overview of the four personality types has been presented, you should be able to identify your own personality style, as well as the style of the prospects you approach. The key is to observe the prospect's behavior, if possible, or to listen to what he or she has to say and how he or she says it. Is the prospect talkative, open, and friendly, or reserved and cautious? Does the prospect ask questions and, if so, are the questions about details or bottom-line results? In short, you must listen and observe intently to learn about prospects. Having learned, you can put that knowledge to good use.

Enthusiasm is key. The bottom line is that when you are enthusiastic about prospecting, it is easy no matter how difficult it may be. Excitement, joy, and an inner feeling of satisfaction permeate the entire activity, stimulating you to put all of your energy and emotions into the project and assuring you that it is probable your objective will be achieved.

How can you become more enthusiastic?

Find your true interest and apply your strength. Do not confuse enthusiasm with noise—shouting or yelling. Dale Carnegie defined enthusiasm as an ardent spiritual quality deep inside—a suppressed excitement.

To be truly excited about prospecting, you must feel a passion for it deep inside yourself. However, you are often required to do things about which you do not have that deep commitment. One way to help develop enthusiasm is to find something connected to the job that you can get excited about. By focusing on this aspect, real enthusiasm will be generated.

EXAMPLE

Emily dreaded the time-consuming job of making follow-up calls to her direct-marketing campaigns. She realized, though, that this was the way to get the most out of mailings. By concentrating on how each successful call would lead her to an interview with a *qualified* prospect, she became enthusiastic about making her way through the list.

Learn as much as you can about prospecting. Learning leads to knowledge, and that knowledge often engenders enthusiasm. The more you know, the more you want to know.

EXAMPLE

When Andrew took over his management position, he dreaded the responsibility of running a weekly meeting. He didn't feel creative enough to make his meetings really effective, and, on reflection, he felt that most of these meetings he'd attended were a waste of time. Still, he was expected to keep up the weekly meeting tradition.

During the next few weeks, Andrew learned as much as he could about how staff meetings could impact the office operation. He spoke with his sales staff and read company and industry texts on meetings, motivation, and training. His attitude about this responsibility changed, and he was challenged each week to put forward his best efforts.

For years, coaches have been giving pep talks to inspire their teams. When your enthusiasm wanes or when you need an extra push to accomplish a mission, give yourself that pep talk.

Keep in mind that great men and women—whether they are in government, business, science, or the arts—possess one common ingredient: enthusiasm about their work and their lives. Beethoven composed his greatest symphonies despite his deafness. Salk refused to give up his search for the cure for polio.

Norman Vincent Peale summed this up as follows: "What goes on in the mind is what determines the outcome. When an individual really gets enthusiastic, you can see it in the flash of the eyes, in the alert and vibrant personality. You can see it in the verve of the whole being. Enthusiasm makes the difference in one's attitude toward other people, toward one's job, toward the world. It makes the big difference in the zest and delight of human existence."

What are your strengths?

Overcoming the Fear of Rejection

Your fear of rejection is your greatest prospecting tool. Learn from rejection. If you don't make that sale, you still have to act. Remember, you learn very little from a sale (most often during a sale, you probably go with the flow and take this type of sale for granted). You learn a lot more from your failures. It's when you don't sell that you ask yourself all kinds of questions: What did I do wrong? Did I make a good presentation? Did I discover the real needs? Why couldn't I overcome the objections? Did I do all that I could have done?

Trying to obtain a sales appointment is as important as selling the product, only it is more difficult, because it's the first step—the point of greatest resistance. If you don't succeed here, you will never get to the presentation or to the close. Once you have the appointment, though, you have a chance. The only way to learn something is to do it. The more you do it, the better you become—it's that simple. So remember: there are two sides to every coin, and there are some positives even from a "no sale."

Some years ago, there was a letter from a disgruntled sales professional in Ann Landers's newspaper column. He was very disappointed in people. "Don't they realize," he asked, "that sales professionals are there to help people? Don't people understand the real value of quality products and services?" He went on to give his own personal experience; he was discouraged to realize that many people don't always understand the good that his products and services offer.

Unfortunately, this sales professional's attitude is quite common. Like so many others, he has failed to understand that human beings don't always know what's good for them. We all want to go to heaven, and yet nobody wants to die. We know smoking is hazardous to our health, and yet millions smoke. We know that safety belts save lives, and yet we need laws to enforce their use. We know we should do this and that, and yet we put what's best for us off till *tomorrow.*

You have to face this truth about the human condition, and you have to understand it. When you apply this understanding to your prospects and customers, you can proceed to find ways to help them decide to act in spite of their hesitancy. That's what selling is all about, whether selling your products or selling your ideas and concepts.

Let's now try to apply these principles to action. Clients will object. They will try not to let you in. They will delay (I have to think about it . . . I have to talk it over with my spouse, lover, friend, whatever). They will hesitate. What are you going to do? Again, it's all a matter of attitude. New sales associates hope to close without objection. Experienced salespeople look for objections, even seek them out. Experienced sales professionals know that once the objection is known, the sale has advanced considerably and chances of closing are excellent.

It's all a question of being prepared and being equipped with the proper attitude, or, as the dictionary defines attitude, with the right *disposition.* Being prepared for the interview is as important as being prepared for the close. As the most successful sales professionals will tell you, the easiest sales happen when you are very well prepared and when you anticipate objections. On the other hand, the most difficult sales are the ones you take for granted. When you take it for granted that a sale will succeed, you are usually *not* prepared. Perhaps it is simply the fact that you don't think you need to prepare—the sale is "in the bag." You don't learn very much when you sell, but you learn a great deal when you don't.

Attitude is a state of mind, the result of all the experiences you have had. Experience teaches us that people's defensive attitudes are normal, natural, even necessary. You learn that people are hesitant to make decisions because they are afraid to make mistakes. For example, millions of people do not marry, not because they don't like the opposite sex, but because they are afraid to make a mistake. The same is true with jobs; millions of individuals who are not happy in their work will not change jobs because they are afraid they might do worse. Once you understand this fear, you can start examining your prospects' other concerns; you can approach your prospects in a different manner. You don't immediately say, "Oh well, they're not interested . . . not very friendly . . . don't like me . . ." You start listening for other messages, such as "Well, I don't know . . . Maybe I should, but . . . I'm afraid to make a mistake . . . Maybe you're not the right salesperson . . . Maybe it's not the best company . . . This isn't the best time . . . I want to wait . . . I want to think it over . . ." On reflection, what we hear them saying is *"You better convince me."*

In these instances, you should try to do exactly the opposite of what prospects expect you to do. Turn the tables, and agree to most of the objections, but still try to get the interview.

Remember, you are not an order taker. You are a sales professional, and in that role your job is to convince people to buy now what they have been wanting to buy for some time. Attitude can turn a negative reaction into a positive one.

It is very difficult to be a top sales professional. Many are called; few succeed. On the other hand, most veterans who have survived appreciate that they can do it. They know that if it *were* easy, the companies and customers they represent would not need them.

The same principle applies in most endeavors. Ask the top professional golfers whether they would want the game of golf to be easier. Of course they wouldn't. If it were easier, everybody could do what they do. The same rule applies for all: *Work hard, practice, and it's your business.* Selling your products and services is your business and, if you are going to survive and succeed in it, you have to work, practice, and continually learn about your business. Because you are dealing with matters that are at times personal, confidential, and emotional, you have to understand human behavior and human attitudes before you can expect success.

The "No" Response

It's easy to say no to just about anything these days. When the economy goes sour, it's a lot easier to turn down requests for donations, raises, expenditures, and just about everything else. No one dares argue in these circumstances. Whatever anyone wants, the answer is "No, no, no!"

Sales professionals understand this new "Just say no" approach. They are hit by it every day. But there's a negative side to saying no too often. It cuts you off from innovative ideas and new ways of doing things.

There are times when saying no isn't so smart. In fact, the desire to avoid sales professionals can keep a prospect from finding out what's happening and what's new.

Here's a simple, six-point guide for getting more prospecting opportunities, seeing more people, and making more sales when everyone seems to be saying no:

1. Be sure you're competent.

There are a lot of people on the streets carrying a salesperson's briefcase who are incompetent. They think they can wing it, live off their charm, and close sales with their flawless techniques. They've done it for the past twenty years, so why change now?

Some younger sales professionals have discovered what these so-called old hands don't understand, and this gives those newer in sales a distinct advantage. Why? Because they are smart enough to know that there are gaps in their knowledge. Such sincerity comes through. If you don't know the answer, be sure to know where you can get it—and be secure enough to let your prospects know what you are going to do.

2. *Know your prospect's business.*

No prospect wants to hear a sales professional say "Can you tell me something about your business?" Why should anyone take the time to educate you on his or her business, just so you can turn around and sell something? If you're in sales, it's your job to know about prospects' business before you try to take their time either on the telephone or in person. If you don't know how to figure out what your prospect's business is, then you shouldn't be in sales.

3. *Be prepared to demonstrate cost savings.*

Forget about talking in vague generalities. Don't bother using examples from your sales book about a business that is in no way comparable to the company you are dealing with at the moment. Buyers want to know how the purchase improves the bottom line. If you can't show cost benefits, you're in trouble—and out the door, where you belong.

4. *Stress quality.*

Prospects want confirmation about you and your company. They may be less concerned with what a product costs than with what your product delivers in value. So now, more than ever, take the time to build your case for quality.

5. Become an educator.

Sales techniques must change with the times. Forget about all the clever techniques that you saw on the latest sales video and the five hundred surefire closes that you memorized so carefully. Clear your mind of that stuff for good. Concentrate instead on ways you can educate your prospects by broadening their under-standing, expanding their knowledge, and opening their eyes to new possibilities.

As you do all this, the prospect comes to the conclusion that you're valuable because you know what you're talking about. This is certainly the very best way to blow away the competition!

6. Be patient.

This is the hardest step of all, particularly at a time when making sales is more difficult than ever. There's a tendency to go to the jugular, go in for the kill, but that's the old way of thinking. *Practice* is the watchword now. Take time. Stay in touch with your prospects. Answer questions. Show genuine interest. Work for them. This is the best way to eventually close a sale.

Getting prospects to say yes instead of no isn't all that easy, but it is possible. It's your job to work on ways to make them un-derstand that by saying no too often, they are actually missing out on valuable opportunities that can benefit their business or personal life.

Chapter 2

Prospecting Strategies, Systems, and Formulas

Prospecting is the key to opening up a market. A prospecting strategy (or system or formula) needs to be carefully fitted to the sales professional's market, as well as to his or her products or services, company, and personal abilities and characteristics. Proven ideas zero in on strategies for making a positive first impression, continuous prospecting, marketing, and client building in a wide array of markets. This chapter details some of the more successful prospecting strategies shared by MDRT sales professionals.

Why Prospects Buy

As a young child, were you required by your parents to learn to play a musical instrument? Perhaps your parents wanted you to learn how to play the piano, and you learned to play the melody on your right hand and later the rhythm with your left. If you the hit the wrong notes, the sound was discordant. Eventually, you learned to blend notes to create harmony. But if you picked the wrong notes, the melody was lost in the noise. You also learned that if you practiced, your playing would improve. The more you practiced, the better you became.

You have heard that "practice makes perfect." You also know that there is a lot of noise in the selling process. This noise occurs when your tune doesn't fit the prospect's harmony.

Realizing that we all would like to harmonize better with our prospective clients, let's explore the human dynamics of selling tangible products and services. It is vitally important to remember that people buy a product or service because they *love* someone or something. So along comes Johnny Salesman, who wants to start talking about the perils of not having a product or service and its affect on the family or business. Guess who is Mr. Popular at the kitchen table? Is it any wonder sales professionals have low self-esteem! They are not exactly seen as spreading merriment and joy or known for the warmth and happiness that they bring to the meeting. There are, of course, those sales professionals who try to mask the fear or pain of loss with jokes, a cheery attitude, enthusiasm, charisma. But eventually, the subject of negative impact must be discussed directly, and that's when the *tension* starts to build.

Seasoned sales professionals recognize the buyer's attitude as based on ignorance and misunderstanding. They write off any tension, animosity, and reluctance to "If they only knew." But sometimes, even when they do know, prospects feel the same way about a product or service and don't buy. As sales professionals leave meetings, dejected and dismayed, they justify their feelings with "Too bad they are so (fill in the blank)." However, too often, sales professionals simply justify their feelings and their prospects' responses without really looking closely at why they failed to make the sale.

The buyer's game has changed. Buyers today are more sophisticated, have more information, more insight. They also have more choices. The selling game has changed as well. Sellers are more sophisticated. They have more technology, more insight, and can offer more choices than ever before. The computer has also changed the sales process to some extent.

Secrets to Sales Success

There are three secrets to successful selling and why people buy. If you can master these three secrets, you can achieve what your mind can conceive.

The first secret is *perspective*. Sales professionals must learn to work *on* the transaction, not *in* it. They have to detach themselves from the selling process to understand what is actually happening for their prospects, which is referred to as the buyer's process.

The second secret has to do with *process*. Sales professionals must develop a repeatable and reliable sales process that they can use in any situation.

The third secret relates to sales professionals' understanding of fundamental *behavioral principles*. Sales professionals must understand who they are and what they stand for. They must project these values and principles to their buyers. If they are incongruent in their beliefs and values, prospects will not trust them.

Let's look at each of these secrets and see what can be learned from them.

At one time or another, you have probably seen or heard of the puzzle of the nine dots. To review briefly, in order to solve the puzzle, you must connect all nine dots with four straight lines. Once you start, you cannot lift the pencil off the paper. However, unless you go outside the square, outside the nine dots, you cannot connect them.

To be successful with this puzzle, you need to create a tenth dot, *a dot of perspective.* You have to remove yourself from the standard way of looking at things and view the problem from a different point of view: perspective. The same is true of selling. Often, sales professionals need to take a different approach when they view a new sales opportunity. Their tenth dot becomes their anchor as they watch the sales process unfold from that dot.

The second secret, *process,* is tied by an umbilical cord to the first secret. Sales professionals have to have a repeatable selling process. They need to know it "cold." There can be no doubt in their minds. They need to be confident and secure in their selling process, otherwise they will never instill confidence in their clients. This is why knowledge is so important.

At the same time, there is also a four-step buyer's process, and you have to become intimately familiar with this as well. You must learn to recognize these four steps each buyer experiences. And here's an extra sales secret. Where is the sale made? In the *fact-finder.*

The third secret, *behavioral principles,* includes three types. There are three sales principles you must learn and use during your career: Whoever says the objection first, owns it. Never ask a question unless you know the answer. You don't have a case until you have a problem. These are fundamentals of the faith, and you must know and understand these important selling rules. And there are two behavioral principles: People buy from the people they like and trust. Objections are merely an expression of their ignorance. Finally, there are life principles, that is, personal values and attitudes you cannot and will not violate. Never lie. When in doubt, tell the truth. Do for others what you would have them do for you. Help others out of a sheer joy of serving.

What do you stand for? Do you know? Write it down.

As a sales professional, you should have three deliverables. The first deliverable is to gain a new perspective on how to *relate* with your clients; the second, to show you the *interrelationship* between the buyer's and the seller's processes; and the third, to give you basic *principles* that will help you become more effective.

Let's look at the selling process. Everything starts in *equilibrium:* the buyers have all of the solutions they need for all of the problems they've got. This is fundamental to selling. If it were any different, the prospect would be seeking a solution right now.

Think about any problem you have right now, something you are dealing with personally. Is it painful? Overbearing? Does it dominate your thoughts? Most likely, you would give anything reasonable to get rid of it. Problems are like that. Most people will do whatever they can to eliminate a problem so they can stop worrying about it.

If that is true, then ask yourself *what* it is that you sell. Do you sell problems? Or do you sell solutions? This question has been asked around the world to many sales professionals, and invariably, more than 90 percent of them say they sell solutions. But do they?

If they sell solutions, then where will the prospect focus—on the cost or the solution? Prospects will mentally weigh the value of the solution compared to the cost. As the cost gets heavier, the solution will become lighter.

If you focus on the *problems,* by helping prospects understand the true nature of their problem and magnitude of the issues they are facing, will they focus on the costs or the problem? More than likely, they will begin to focus on the problem. The heavier the problem, the lighter the cost.

To grow your business, you must be *known* by the problems you solve, not the solutions you sell. That does not mean you should not be an expert in solutions. Of course not! But you must learn to focus on the problems and reinforce these problems in the mind of the client.

Your goal must be to *facilitate* solutions for your clients, but only after they fully grasp the depth and magnitude of their problems. So ask yourself, why do people buy? The bottom line is that *they buy because they want to.* If you remember nothing else, remember that people do what they want to do, when they want to do it.

This all starts with a selling process: a series of sequential steps that are followed to a predictable end result. You must follow these with diligence.

All sales professionals know that nothing happens until they find a prospect. You must then present a well-reasoned argument for why prospects should do business with you. The opening interview should result in nothing more than an agreement to allow you to review a prospect's current circumstances and to offer a second opinion on a plan of action. Anything else could be interpreted as overselling, and you run the risk of losing the opportunity to do business with your prospect. After all, if an aggressive sales professional tries to close a sale on you on the first interview, how do you feel?

MDRT studies of member sales results show that 87 percent of all fact-finders result in a sale. If you knew that 87 percent of the time, your efforts would result in a sale, what would you concentrate on doing? Opening a good case? All you have to do is convince your prospect to allow you to gather the facts. Yet, evidence shows that the number of opening interviews are dropping. Sales professionals are spending too little time practicing their opening interview. Yet, this is where it all happens. If you cannot convert an opening interview into a fact-gathering meeting, you have either done a poor job of prospecting, not established your credibility, or poorly reasoned your opening logic.

Clearly, if you want to increase your selling success, it all starts with the opening interview. Here are three keys:

1. Obtain an agreement on a *vital issue.*

2. Create a *critical idea* in the mind of your prospect.

3. Demonstrate a *process* to develop alternative solutions.

A vital issue could be the long-term impact of purchasing your products or services. A critical idea is to empower prospects to take action. Demonstrate that they can actually find a solution to their problem. By demonstrating a sales process, you show prospects that you have thoughtfully considered the logic of your process and can effectively communicate steps that lead to your conclusions.

A well-reasoned opening interview is worth the time and energy required to make your case. If you do this properly, you position yourself for the fact-finder. The sale is always made in the fact-finder.

So, how do you become more efficient? Pretend for a moment that you possess a magic box. This magic box will produce unlimited amounts of money from unlimited amounts of paper that you systematically feed into the slot. If you had a magic box like this, what would you do? Obviously, you would put as much paper into the box as possible. Unfortunately, one day, your machine stops producing money. Now what? Fix it? The box is hermetically sealed. No one can fix it. All you can do is wait for it to heal.

What could be wrong? Could it be the paper? The wrong bond, wrong grade, wrong weight? Perhaps it was the flow; perhaps you were putting paper into the box too fast.

Eventually, your box does come back to life, but very slowly. It starts to produce small amounts of money again. Now that it is producing money again, what should you do to protect your magic box? First, you need to make certain you are putting good paper into the box; second, you should control the flow of paper. But how do you develop consistency to protect your magic box? You need a filter, something that would warn you that you are about to damage your magic box.

Your sales process needs a filter, too. Each of you has a magic box right now in your possession. That fact is beyond question. What is in doubt is only *how much* it will produce. You are limited by your prospects and your people skills. Once you master those two elements, you are on your way to life-long success.

What is the biggest mistake you've made in sales? For many sales professionals, it's a lack of discernment. Most sales professionals who are new in the business go anywhere, at any-time, and any place to find prospects. But some only go if they have a good idea that prospects might buy. They have no real plan, just a list of characteristics they are looking for in a client—sort of like a profile, but they wouldn't say "no" to some-one if they thought they could help them.

You need a profile of the prospects who you are looking for. It's been said that if you don't know where you are going, any place will do. Prospecting is like that. You can waste your most precious resource—time—if you don't know who you are trying to see. Many sales professionals have a file full of clients they will never call on again. Is this bad? It's how they survive. But eventually, they have to change their market and how they invest their time.

Here's how a filter works. It matches your most successful selling style with your most successful sales opportunities. Go back and look at your last twenty sales. Maybe you have to look at your last forty sales. Which ones were the most successful? What were the common denominators? Somewhere in your re-cent history, there is a pattern of success that, if you could only duplicate it, would multiply your sales results.

The Buyer's Process

As mentioned earlier, there is also a buyer's process. The buyer is going through a series of thoughts and fears at the same time you are introducing your critical issue. When you first make the approach, it is adversarial. Buyers are not waiting with open arms to purchase a product from you. They may recognize they need some help, but until you establish your credentials and trustworthiness, they will stand back and wait.

It's important to note that there is a four-step process that all prospects go through when they consider buying a product or ser-vice. Regardless of whether one is talking about a one-interview sale or a series of interviews that culminates in a sale, the process is always the same.

Step 1 is *denial*. Prospects have no clue they have a problem. If they do know, then either they have had some coaching or they have intuitively begun to realize their vulnerability. If they actually grasp the problem, they have probably already taken steps to solve it.

Denial usually sounds like an objection: I don't need it, I can't afford it, I already have enough, my brother sells life insurance, and any other objection you have ever heard. These objections stem from ignorance. We *like* ignorance. We *like* denial. Denial means prospects haven't started to address these issues and so you have the opportunity to provide real service, to bond with them. It provides you with the chance to educate them and lead them out of the darkness, into the light.

The initial phase of your selling process has to mesh with prospects' buying process. If you move prospects through denial too fast, they will think less of your process and not fully understand your value. This is why the one-interview sale does not work with large-case prospects. Unless prospects are looking specifically for an identified solution, you need to take them through a process to a logical conclusion.

Perhaps you have heard of the concept of the "deal before the deal." This is the second filter and a very important part of your selling process. It is how you close the opening interview. You must have the courage to walk away from prospects who will never buy from you. Think of the last sale you lost. When did you know you were going to lose it? Most sales professionals say they know early in the process, maybe during the first interview. Yet, they have this interminable self-confidence that if they say the right thing, show the right numbers, and pick the right time to ask for the order, they will ultimately make the sale. In reality, this is rarely true. In fact, they often end up putting the wrong paper in their magic box and nothing ever comes out the other end.

The opening interview is all about denial. You must have a repeatable selling idea that can be used in all circumstances to move prospects to the next phase in your process.

Step 2 is *enlightenment.* The prospect has begun to understand the scope of his or her problem and is becoming aware of the related price tag. Enlightenment has two phases: understanding the alternatives and understanding the consequences. Sales professionals who do not allow prospects to process the consequences have missed the most powerful selling tool in their arsenal.

Some sales professionals have learned their best lessons about selling the hard way. Says one sales professional, "Our two oldest children were admitted to a drug/alcohol rehabilitation center when they were 14 and 16. It was then that I made the most important discovery about human behavior, namely, people do what they want to do when they want to do it."

The fact-finder phase is all about enlightenment. Bringing your clients to the place where they fully understand their circumstances requires great skill and patience. You must ask questions and listen to their answers. By carefully asking the right questions and then helping them process their circumstances you can lead them to a full understanding of their choices.

Let's look at some of the things you can do during the fact-finder to build trust and lead your client to enlightenment.

First, differentiate between hard facts and soft facts. Hard facts are all about who owns what and what goes where. Frankly, this is the least important aspect of the fact-finder. It is merely a snapshot of your prospect's current financial situation.

The soft facts make the sale. These questions have to do with who prospects love, why they have made decisions in the past, what they really care about and want to see happen. You must seek the meaning behind the meaning. What are the hidden objections?

Once you complete the fact-finder, you then enter the design phase of the selling process. The design phase is really an iteration between design and presentation. You must show your prospects a variety of alternative solutions in a professional and understandable manner. Ultimately, they will come to a place where they are forced to choose between two or three choices: your product or service or the alternative choices. Whatever the consequences, they must internalize them and ultimately make a decision.

This is when step 3 of the buyer's process occurs. The key to the sale happens when the *pain* of making these choices becomes unavoidable. This is the step in the selling process most sales professionals miss. Look at this as a grieving process. In a general sense, the grieving process has several steps that have been discussed in various articles, books, and speeches. Basically, there is a period of mourning and grief, then resignation, anger, and finally acceptance. Grief is the key to eventually healing the emotional wound. If one has not adequately grieved over the death of a loved one, then the emotional healing will be indefinitely postponed.

Major purchasing decisions are painful processes, too. Agreeing that your product or service is the best solution requires a grieving period. The prospect has to adequately internalize the problem and then accept the natural consequences before he or she can accept what you offer as the best solution. This internalization is a grieving process, just like accepting death.

What do you think will happen if the grieving period is cut short by overzealous sales professionals who stop the process by giving their prospects answers too soon? Do you think their prospects will be ready to hear solutions? Where will prospects focus their attention—on the *pain* or the *solution?* Even if your solution is the best option for their situation, if prospects are not ready for it, they will not buy it.

How many times have you experienced the frustration or heard other sales professionals express anger over blown deals, when prospects give all the buying signals and sales professionals, who have gathered minimal facts, jump on the opportunity? They then begin to demonstrate how their products or services will help prospects. They think they have sales at hand and start spending their commissions. Prospects decide to (pick one): wait; shop around; do nothing; think about it; talk to professional associate, friend, mother-in-law, other; buy something similar. It is always the same, if the grieving is not complete. People only buy when they feel they have no other viable alternative.

Your selling process is very much like a grieving process, and you have to allow for this process to fully take shape. The design/presentation iteration is really a *negotiation* between you and your prospects. You are showing them all their alternatives while they are trying to find the best solution. As long as you allow them to grieve over their alternatives, you will virtually always make a sale.

The ideal circumstance is when the prospect says to you, "Wouldn't your product or service work here?" Do you think you could close that sale? When prospects fully process their alternatives, they move into the final step of the buyer's process. Step 4 is the *implementation* phase.

We know that buyers buy because they want to. When was the last time you ever did anything you didn't want to do? Prospects buy because they think what you sell is the best solution for their circumstances. If prospects are making the purchase, it is not because they have a gun to their heads. They would stop themselves from paying you if they really didn't want what you have to offer. Life is usually about gratification. Most people only do what they really want to do, when they want to do it.

You need to *time* your process to the buyer's process. At the same time, you need to be sensitive to your prospect's emotional development. To push prospects too soon dooms the sale. You want a soft landing. This occurs when prospects decide or need to do something at the same time you are ready to present a viable solution. This is when the harmony of the effort becomes a symphony of sound. Discord is noise. But if everyone is on pitch and in the same key, you have beautiful music.

You can learn to harmonize with your prospects and buyers simply by waiting until they have completed their buying cycle. Your challenge is to master the tell-tale signs and then develop the patience to allow them to come to the proper conclusion on their own. Good sales professionals are sensitive to their prospects' process and can time their own selling process to the emotional swings their prospects will experience. Learn to recognize the buyer's process and you will improve your productivity.

Keep Customers Coming Back and Prospects Begging for More

Picture this: You're in your office and the phone rings. It's Daniel, one of your good clients. Daniel says, "I've been thinking. It's time for me to buy (he names one of your products), and I want you to meet my friend so he too can see what you have to offer." You say, "Sounds like a good idea. How about Thursday, at 2 P.M.? You stop by with your friend, and we'll take care of your needs and your friend's needs as well."

You no sooner hang up the phone, and it rings again. This time it's Andrew, an acquaintance you met at the health club. He too wants to talk about purchasing some of your products and services. You tell him you would more than happy to see him on Friday at 11 A.M.

If this happens to you on a regular basis, congratulations! Then the goal of this section is to help you identify why it's happening so that you can keep it happening. If this is still a dream of yours, then the goal is to help you identify the steps you need to take to make it a reality. You probably know sales associates who you believe have this kind of day, one where the prospects and clients are lined up to see them. One of the reasons you believe this is that you see these outstanding individuals involved in their industry, active in community affairs, spending time with their families, traveling, pursuing personal interests. If they have time to do all that and they're so successful in generating business, then the clients and prospects must be coming to them, wouldn't you say?

So, what do these people and other highly successful sales professionals have in common?

The first thing to notice is that they know where they are going, and they're highly focused on what it is that they must do each day, for today's business and for the future. (Don't worry, they have the same interruptions we all do, the same decision to make with "more choices than when I got out of bed," and the same occasional doubts about whether this is the best way to do things. But they seem to be on a mission every day, with a clear idea of the most important thing to accomplish right now.)

They're well-rounded, balanced individuals, because they've identified their priorities and make sure they invest part of themselves in each important area of their lives. To do this, they delegate well and surround themselves with highly competent specialists in areas that complement their own strengths. They put things on "automatic" by having a system that runs their day, and their assistants and other staff have a system that runs the balance of their organization. They also have respectful relationships with other professionals who serve their clients.

In addition, they share their success with others, both in their industry and in their community. They take care of their best clients personally and have a support system to handle the rest. They are continually marketing, in their own unique ways, and appear not to have to do any traditional prospecting at all.

In short, they are good folk, good sales professionals, have good business sense, and they are smart marketers! Yes, you heard right: marketers. But what exactly is marketing? Although selling and marketing are directly connected and overlap in many ways, they are not the same thing. Marketing is everything you do to put yourself in front of a qualified prospect or client, over and over again. Selling is what you do to help your prospect identify a problem and choose a solution that you recommend.

Ray Willsmer, a Canadian educator, in 1979 wrote a book titled *Marketing: A Guide to Increasing Profits.* In it he says, "Marketing is an awareness of what you are doing, why you are doing it, and what the implications are—now and in the future." Business ethics and your personal moral code are a big part of that, and remain so no matter what you do to market yourself.

There's another message here. Marketing underlies everything you do in business. The better marketer you are, the better chance you have of keeping your clients coming back and your prospects begging to buy. So you must have a marketing plan! We know that it's important to have a marketing plan, but frankly, most salespeople have not prepared an in-depth plan in the past year, if at all! Unless you need financing for your business, there's just not enough incentive to go through the onerous process.

"It isn't necessary to answer five hundred questions [to have an effective business plan]," writes Willsmer. "The replies to only six questions, the same ones Kipling used, will provide most of the benefit any business may be seeking. As a matter of fact, dealing with only the six basic questions is often far better."

Rudyard Kipling's six questions are contained in this sonnet:

> I keep six honest serving men
> (They taught me all I know).
> Their names are WHAT and WHY and WHEN
> And WHERE and WHO and HOW.

So, let's take that approach. Ask yourself the who, what, where, why, when, and how questions. The answers all tie together somehow, and asking them will bring you insights that will be immediately beneficial to you and your clients.

The Cream of the Crop

Who are your best clients? You probably have an intuitive sense about who they are, and about the answers to the rest of these questions too. But take this exercise beyond just the gut level to really look at your client files.

If you have a computerized database of clients, your assistant can prepare a printout and initial analysis of where your business is coming from. Then you can look at it more in depth, by asking yourself not only who has given you the most business so far, including their own checks and the referrals they've sent you, but who has the potential to continue to do so in the future. If your client list is not computerized, then you might refer to your commission statements as a starting point, then to the actual client files to learn more about them.

Make a list of your best twenty clients, so you know who you should be nurturing at any time. What do they have in common? What clubs or organizations do they belong to? What professions are they in? What neighborhoods do they live in? Do they have children? Grandchildren? What about their sphere of influence? Have you been able to tap into it for referrals?

Nurture these top client relationships in a manner that's appropriate to each. Some need more personal attention; others need your expertise and your direction, quickly. Some would appreciate a lunch meeting, others just a quick fifteen-minute meeting to make decisions and the balance of the time working behind the scenes. The amount of time you spend with any specific client is not in direct proportion to the business he or she gives you.

It's not the amount of time you spend with your clients that makes the difference, it's the quality of that time. And quality is measured by the client, from his or her own perspective. Your job is to intuit what kind of relationship the client needs, and deliver it. And you get better with experience.

What are you selling, and what is the client buying? Are the answers to both questions the same? If not, what business are you really in?

Why do your clients buy from you? Part of the answer may be just that you were in the right place at the right time. And that comes from an intuitive sense of timing and from being in the prospect's mind most of the time. But you can't be everywhere all the time, so it's a good idea to ask your clients, "What is it that made you buy from me and makes you stay with us?"

Are you a bit nervous about asking these questions? Don't worry. The worst thing that will happen is that you'll get an earful about a problem they're experiencing with your service. That gives you an opportunity to make things right and save your clients, instead of having them tell a competitor the same thing and take their business elsewhere.

The best thing that will happen when you ask these questions is that you'll find the real hot buttons, the real reasons for buying, and the unique position you and your organization hold in the mind of your clients. This can become the basis of your mission statement: using that word or group of words that come naturally from your client's mouth when describing you and your services.

How did your clients learn about your services? Was it word-of-mouth? Was it an article you had written in a publication that your clients read? Was it a referral? An ad? A seminar you conducted? You may have known about your client long before he or she became aware of you. You may have courted the client as a prospect, with or without the client's conscious knowledge.

When was the first appointment with this client? Under what circumstances was this appointment made? When did the client finally trust you enough to do business with you?

With most clients, there may have been many contacts before you actually made the sale. What's important is which of those contacts the client believes was the first, and which the most significant, in his or her initial relationship with you. People act on their perception of reality, not on the facts of reality.

Where can you find other prospects like your best clients? Usually, your clients are your best prospects, and referrals from your clients and other centers of influence are your second-best prospects. Being clear about what makes a good client for you is a critical first step in getting the right kind of referrals. Third best are prospects whose profile closely matches that of your best clients.

It was easy fifty years ago to answer the W,W,W,W,W, and H questions. Back then, sales professionals had territories assigned to them, limited product lines, requirements to see each person in their territories a certain number of times each year, and a sales reporting system that allowed them to answer most of these questions with just a little research. The biggest concern was that they didn't have total control of their target market, because the company could change their territory at will.

Times have changed. Now most sales professionals must choose and develop their own territories, choose what products they will sell, decide whom to see and how often and set up their own database to track information about their clients and their own activities, and decide how to keep in touch when they can't be there personally.

Therein lies a big difference. The choices afforded us by advancements in computer technology have changed the way we sell. Everything from direct mail to online marketing to multifaceted products has become possible in the past two decades because of these advancements. So, how can you take advantage of this new potential? How can you decide what steps to take next?

Exploring some of the options, looking at how to evaluate their importance in your business, and then choosing the one(s) that will be most productive for you to use right now will help you decide what to do to put your plan into action.

The following options are in alphabetical order for your convenience.

Advertising

If you want to determine the value of advertising for your business, just recall the number of people in your industry who have used ads, billboards, and so on to promote themselves, and how few are still doing it. That's because advertising can be expensive and can have two different purposes.

The first type of advertising is intended to get an immediate response from your audience. An example of this is an ad for a seminar that you are sponsoring. This type of ad needs a big benefit statement, a sense of urgency, and an easy way for readers to register right now.

The second type of advertising is awareness advertising. This must be carefully targeted and used in situations where you are most likely to attract the kind of prospects you're seeking. Ads in local business magazines, in special editions, or in an edition that contains an article by you are good examples of awareness advertising. Others include sponsoring a local Little League team, school choir, charitable golf tournament, or cultural event. These are spin-offs of life-long commitments that you have made to your community, and only make sense if they are logical extensions to the work and involvement you already have. You can't buy your way in if you aren't already on the inside.

Unfortunately, most advertising takes so long to build the awareness you need that it has little short-term impact. And it can be costly, not only in terms of ad space, but in the personal effort and other resources needed to prepare a good ad. It's better to think of everything you do as being your personal form of advertising.

Articles for Publication

Publishing your own articles or a regular column in a well-targeted magazine or other publication is a very positive positioning tool, if it's done well. Most publishers/editors do not have time to edit your material, and they certainly don't have the knowledge of your profession and its legal obligations (if applicable) that is required to edit properly. If you produce your own material, it is your responsibility to deliver ready-made articles that are thoroughly sourced and error-free. If you purchase or rent material to use, then insist on evidence of sources and reliability.

Don't start a column unless you know you'll be able to continue to provide material on a regular basis. Prepare several columns ahead, so that you won't get caught with nothing ready at deadline time. Get agreement in writing from the publication's editor that none of the content will be changed without your express written permission, and make sure that there is a way for the reader to reach you, if there is some immediate interest. Include an offer of some free information if a reader calls, for example, a copy of another timely article, a free checklist, or something else that would be useful to your clients.

It is not necessary to have a weekly or even a monthly column. Four times a year is plenty in terms of workload, and the frequency doesn't matter as much as the regularity and reliability. Have reprints of your article made, either by the publisher or by your own printer, so you can use them in client and prospect servicing, as well as for continuing development of centers of influence.

One way to develop material for your column is to be the column sponsor, introducing the works of other professionals with whom you might work. This makes you an editor rather than a writer, and can become a burden or a blessing, depending on your skills and talents and the reliability of those who are submitting articles to you for publication.

Whether you do the writing or someone else does it, it's important to prepare some guidelines concerning the type of articles, the intended audience, the type of examples (i.e., real clients or hypothetical cases), how long the articles will be, the use of graphs and other illustrations, and so on.

If, as with 99.9 percent of others in your profession, your top priorities and unique abilities do not include writing your own material, then here are a few ideas for sources for edited and approved articles:

One or more of your sponsoring companies or suppliers. Advance marketing articles from these sources can be good, but often have a different slant than you would like. They are usually geared toward you instead of your client, and sometimes require that you use the byline of the person who wrote it rather than your own byline.

Previously published materials. Sometimes, you'll read an article that you really like in a publication other than the one where you want your column to appear. Many of us have clipped such articles and sent them on to specific clients or centers. Remember that you do not own that material and must get appropriate permission from the copyright owner before using it in any form other than as a clipping. You must also comply with whatever criteria the copyright owner requires. This usually takes the form of a credit at the end of your article, stating, "This material has been reprinted with permission from the XYZ edition of the CCC publication," or whatever the copyright owner requires.

Your publisher. If you already have a newsletter publisher providing you with personalized client newsletters, you may be able to negotiate terms under which you can reprint selected articles from your newsletters. Remember again, that you don't own these articles and must abide by the conditions of their use, including "rental" fees and appropriate credit where required.

A ghostwriter. You can always hire your own ghostwriter for this and other marketing materials that you need. Over time, a good writer will learn about your business and how you operate, and can become quite self-sufficient in anticipating and preparing what you need. With the growing home business industry, freelancers are becoming more readily available. Be prepared to invest in a learning curve for both you and the writer. Make sure you have a contract that states who owns the copyright on the materials used, and who else your ghostwriter may have as a client while working with you.

Audio or Video Business Cards

These require a significant investment of your time and your money, so check with someone you know who is using them to find out what's involved and what the actual results are. One of the biggest benefits of using an audio or video business card is that you must do the strategic thinking necessary to determine what to say to your listener, and you are guided through that process by professionals who have learned what the key questions and processes are to do this.

Because businesses do change and grow constantly, it pays to think in advance about how you would deal with any change in partnership, address, phone number, or even business specialty in which you are currently engaged. Here are tips to make sure that your big investment isn't spoiled by missing out on thinking about some of the details in advance:

Focus on your unique service to your clients rather than on any specific product.

In case you move or change phone numbers during the life of your program, include your phone number on the label of the cassette (where it can be changed) rather than in the audio or video portion. If you do use your phone number in your voice message, and you subsequently move or change your numbers, make sure there's a trail for anyone who calls you at the old number. Position the address and phone number so that an attractive label can be placed over it rather than having to design and print another multicolor cover to do the same job. Refer to the fact that you work well with other professionals (either your own associates or those of your clients), rather than mentioning any specific names.

Birthday and Greeting Cards

Most people love to receive birthday cards and greeting cards of any kind. If your card is one that your clients receive, then it's one of very few. That makes it a great way to be remembered.

Brochures

How many times have you said to yourself, "I wish I had a brochure or something to send when people ask about what I do, or when I'm introducing myself to a new referral!" Few salespeople are in a position to have all of their materials, including letterhead, business cards, and other stationery, custom-designed for them. Most salespeople would do well to use a template that has already been proven successful and have their materials prepared by a company that specializes in that, particularly if the supplier is a specialist in the industry.

Computerized Communication Systems

Let's face it, everyone has a contact management system of some kind. And despite all the talk about technology, many of the most successful salespeople are still without a personal computer and yet have little trouble remembering their top clients and associates. If this sounds like you, you and your staff have a real treat in store when you discover how quickly you can communicate with anyone around the world through e-mail and fax modem. You'll also be able to maintain all kinds of data about your clients, including their birthdays and anniversaries and the names of those who referred them to you, as well as referrals they've given you.

And we've all heard of database marketing and how important it is to work the names that have already done business with you. This is almost impossible to do without a computerized database.

An excellent book to open your eyes to the potential of computerized communication is *Strategic Marketing for the Digital Age* by Bill Bishop. It's easy to browse and read and contains no extraneous technolanguage.

Direct-Mail Marketing

There are two ways to look at direct marketing. Most people immediately think of cold, prospecting mailings to a purchased list—in other words, lead generation. But direct marketing is also what you do when you send mailings to your clients when you have important information for them, for instance, at year end to appraise their needs, or to announce changes in your services or in issues affecting their purchases. The difference is in the degree of personalization for each recipient.

Your success is dependent on the quality of the list, the effectiveness of the communication piece used, and the follow-up after the mailing.

Lead generation has proven successful for many agents, either as the primary source of prospects or to supplement the referrals and repeat business generated elsewhere. One example of direct-mail marketing is the salesperson who mails out fifty letters each week, then follows up with phone calls. Are you familiar with a few salespeople who've continued this practice throughout their careers? The key is their follow-up calls.

For many, direct mail is used only for warm contacts: clients and others with whom they've already spoken and have some kind of relationship. It's a form of keeping in touch rather than just a quick qualifier.

Gift Giving

Do you love giving gifts? You should, because you will find that a gift can really knock the socks off your clients. Here are a few examples of what clients appreciate if you choose to give them gifts at any time:

> Clients love receiving good *books* that help them in their business or personal effectiveness, especially if you include a note pointing out a special chapter or section that you think would be of particular interest. If possible, keep a supply of publishers' remainders on hand for gift giving. These are hardcover books that have gone into paperback and are now being sold as remainders at very good prices. Use these as spontaneous gifts, to say thank you for a referral or a suggestion that helps you to improve your service, or to say thanks for understanding when you've had unhappy clients and fixed the problem for them.

> If you ever have any special client events, send those who attended copies of the *photos or videos* that you take of them. Clients love that! In fact, any excuse to have photos taken with clients and then send them a copy is a good one. Also, give them *awards* sometimes, as a thank you for being great clients. Just take a look at what's displayed in most sales professional's offices (maybe even in yours): photos, awards, posters. One of them might as well be yours.

And then there's the MDRT sales professional who has a very special gift that he gives to clients who continually make large purchases with him. These VIPs receive a Mont Blanc Serpent pen, rare, beautiful, and not likely ever to be forgotten. It's a prestige thing. It invites conversation when seen in someone's shirt or jacket pocket or on the desk. This sales professional notes that he saw both of his top clients at a funeral recently, and one asked the other, "So, have you got one of his serpent pens, too?"

Marketing by Fax

Marketing by fax is an effective way to keep your clients informed of events that might interest them, ideas that might help them, and changes that might affect them and require some action on their part. A few words of caution:

Most people don't appreciate unsolicited prospecting faxes, so make sure your clients don't object to this method of contact.

Using a nighttime fax service to save money and avoid tying up business lines during the day can be beneficial, but it can also backfire. In one instance, a salesperson sent a fax blitz to alert his clients of a change in product information, and had several complaints because many had offices at home, and the fax ringing woke up the household. So, limit the faxing to a reasonable time of day or evening, or segregate your fax list to make sure you don't get into trouble.

Choose a fax cover according to your style. If you are faxing from a computer, the fax software will most likely contain standard fax cover sheets, some quite comical, and you can scan your own logo into your system to create a personalized cover page. This is best left to an assistant who can prepare the cover sheets, then show you how to use them.

To save time and paper at the receiving end, incorporate your entire message into one page and forget the cover sheet entirely.

Never fax information of a confidential nature without first calling to make sure the recipient is standing by.

There is an entire chapter on marketing by fax in *Marketing Magic,* edited by Rick Crandall. The book also contains a chapter on client newsletters, one on online marketing, and chapters on other specific marketing issues.

Newsletters

A newsletter is still one of the best and most versatile marketing tools you can use. Newsletters are excellent for client service and for building relationships with future clients. They position you as the person to call in your area of expertise, making it easier to get appointments and referrals, and can be used effectively in a telemarketing operation as well as by the individual producer.

Having your newsletter published and printed by a newsletter service is the quickest way to get the job done right. Choose a publisher who meets your needs, with a selection of articles that suits your business. Make it as turnkey as is practical, given any personalization that you wish to do at your own end.

Turn your newsletter into a proactive tool for getting appointments by asking "Which articles appealed to you the most?" Make it a referral-generator by asking "Who would appreciate a copy of my newsletter?"

Online Marketing

Online marketing includes everything from Web pages to e-mail to fax modem messages and even voice messages on the Internet. Will your personal Web page produce direct business for you? Not likely, but depending on your market and your area of expertise, it may position you well.

Perhaps a Web page is not necessary right now, but e-mail and fax modem capabilities are another thing entirely. Whether you personally operate the computer or not, these two functions can provide incredible improvements in the efficiency and effectiveness of your communications.

E-mail and fax modem messages are quicker to produce and send than regular typed messages. They require less editing because of the more informal language that's the norm on the Internet and in fax notes. No printouts are required unless you need a copy with you at a presentation, and files can be easily stored in the computer by client name and date. Most computerized contact-management systems have an e-mail and fax messaging capability when combined with some standard fax modem and communications software such as WinFax or WinComm Pro.

In one case, a client asked to use a MDRT sales professional's newsletters on his Web page. The sales professional asked him why a local service provider like himself would want to have a World Wide Web presence. His answer: "Since setting up my computer on the Internet, I no longer make house calls. All my clients come to my office, because here is where I have access to all the information they need. Often, clients will tell me that they buy 'this or that' from someone. I just look up that company's Web page, see what they're recommending, and tell clients that I can process their order right now, if they wish! Whether I am able to help them plan and choose otherwise, or simply implement a decision they've already made, it cements my relationship with them, and makes it easier to get them to call me next time before making a decision."

Referral Systems

Research indicates that prospects who were approached through a referral close twice as easily, buy more in the first two years, and stay with a salesperson or company longer than other forms of leads.

Focus on referrals and you'll also improve your persistence, for two reasons. Clients more readily give you referrals when they're happy with your work, and they feel a stronger commitment to you when they know their friends and associates are also doing business with you.

Dan Sullivan's *The Strategic Coach* specifies referability habits that make a lot of sense as a base for making yourself referable:

✓ Do what you say you'll do.

✓ Show up on time.

✓ Finish what you start.

✓ Say "please" and "thank you."

In addition, if you can refer people (and ideas) to your clients and centers, they'll be more receptive to referring others to you. Be clear about what kind of referral you're looking for, and plan for and prepare yourself to ask for referrals as a regular part of your routine with clients. Here are some good times to ask:

✓ When a client agrees to purchase your products or services and gives you the first payment.

✓ When you deliver a product or service.

✓ When you are complimented about your service.

✓ Any time you can create a good reason.

If you haven't already developed a positioning statement that makes it easy for you to lead into asking for a referral (and qualify the names at the same time), then the sample form in Figure 2.1 might help you keep the description of your best clients in the front of your mind, so that when you ask for a referral, you always get the best kind for your business.

To use this positioning statement most effectively, you'll need to do two things. First, clearly identify your best market, in the context of the person from whom you're requesting the referral. Second, use language that helps the listener paint a picture in his or her mind of whom you'd like to meet. According to Joe Girard, deemed one of the world's greatest sales professionals (that's marketing for you!), each person knows and has some influence over the decisions of about 250 other people. The idea is to get the names of some of those people (the right ones) first on the tip of the tongue of your client, then written down as a referral for you. Avoid industry jargon in your "magic phrase," and don't make your listener qualify the prospect too much with your

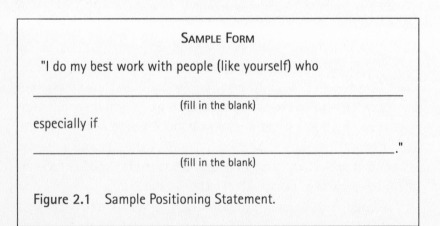

SAMPLE FORM

"I do my best work with people (like yourself) who

_____
                    (fill in the blank)
especially if
                                                     ."
_____
                    (fill in the blank)

Figure 2.1   Sample Positioning Statement.

first question. An example of the wrong way to use this phrase is, "I do my best work with people who have lots of money, especially if they'd be willing to invest some of that with me."

Don't laugh! It's not uncommon for this to be the first thing a sales professional thinks of. Now, if this works for you, don't change it. But if you'd like to improve your referral-generating ability, use these as better examples:

✓ "I do my best work with family-owned businesses, especially if the owner has been talking about cutting back on his or her involvement in the business."

✓ "I do my best work with people like you who are active in their community, especially if they sit on one or more boards of directors."

Now that you've got your client thinking about someone that you might like to meet, take the next step and get the referral's name on the table. This "magic phrase" was first developed to be used in conjunction with a client newsletter, and then followed with the question, "Who do you know (who fits this description) who might appreciate a copy of my newsletter?" But you can follow up with, "Who do you know, someone like yourself, who might benefit from talking with me?"

Telemarketing

In many people's minds, telemarketing is simply a numbers game: call enough people and you'll get the number of appointments you want. But with this attitude, many salespeople have had bad experiences using strangers to promote their business on the telephone.

It would be natural for your assistant to set an appointment on your behalf or to call and pass on some information that you may not be able to handle because of other commitments. Both of these activities could be considered forms of telemarketing, albeit specific to the situation. The term telemarketing is made up of two parts: *tele,* which refers to the telephone, and *marketing,* which is anything you do to get your products and services into the hands of your clients and keep them there.

Some salespeople use telemarketing as a form of lead generation early in their careers. Others who have become very successful have used telemarketing to avoid losing touch with their markets while they're personally focusing on their top clients, and to help with fundraising projects that keep them involved in their community.

Here are a few tips to improve whatever use of telemarketing you make in your business, whether it's you, your assistant, or another professional telemarketer who makes the calls:

✓ Be clear about the purpose of each call. If your purpose is to get an appointment, stay focused and don't try to sell the product over the phone. If it's to raise money for a favorite charity, make sure that's the focus of the call.

✓ Prepare for each call. Using a script as a guideline is the best way to make sure you anticipate what to say, what questions may be asked, and how to respond to them.

✓ Have all the information you'll need organized at the phone for quick access. This includes an appointment schedule with open areas blocked off and an indication of what part of the city you'll be in at that time.

✓ Choose a telemarketer who understands your business and the language needed to communicate effectively with your clients and prospects. Listen while calls are being made to make sure you feel comfortable with the approach being used and to provide initial coaching.

Wild and Crazy Ideas

Sometimes, sales professionals are inspired to do some wild and crazy things. Once in a while, they backfire; most of the time, they don't do much except get a few people talking for a little while. But sometimes they work.

One wild and crazy idea was carried out by a sales professional who handed out "I've been hugged" stickers at trade shows. This sales professional reported that the response was great! In fact, she more than doubled the number of leads from trade shows, and has since discovered that some clients think of those "hug stickers" as her trademark.

Word-of-Mouth Marketing

Statistics show that for every person who has something positive to say about your service, there could be as many as eleven who have something negative to say.

Word-of-mouth marketing goes on all the time, but it's often out of your control. What you can do is make sure that every encounter with the outside world is a positive one, and when a mistake is made, that the solution you provide to make it right again is worth talking about positively.

If you'd like to turn word-of-mouth marketing into an active campaign, pick up Jerry R. Wilson's book by the same name. It shows how to turn this whole area into a skill to be mastered.

Turning Ideas into Results

Now that you've had a refresher on what works, how do you decide where to focus your own marketing efforts next and create your own unique marketing strategy? The best way to decide what to do now is to picture where you'll be at some point down the road—three years from now, one year from now, ninety days from now. Then ask yourself, "How did I get there?"

Create a spreadsheet to evaluate marketing methods to use in the future. List what you're already doing and your level of satisfaction with each facet of your marketing. Then list the things that you would like to do but are not currently doing. In both cases, score each item on a scale of one to ten, one not being very important or productive, and ten being extremely important and potentially productive.

Next, mark beside each item whether it is a short-term strategy or a long-term one (S or T will suffice). Indicate beside each top-ranking item the result you want and the resources needed and available to carry out such a method.

By now, you've probably decided which methods you want to use, so set the direction and get someone else to implement it for you. Identify the coach or mentor you'll work with and the supplier or staff person who will manage the process, and establish some dates by which certain things should be achieved and evaluated. Communicate your vision and your expectations to those who will develop and implement the processes.

So, the message is:

✓ Know what business you're in and who your best clients are.

✓ Keep doing what's working, and add to your marketing mix only what makes sense for you to do. Ideas are a dime a dozen (or less). Only implemented ideas stand a chance of working.

Ready? Set. Go! Now, practice your new skills until they become part of the way you do business. It's just one more step in the direction of keeping clients coming back and prospects begging to buy.

Locating and Qualifying Prospects

Sales professionals must have prospects. You cannot sell unless you have someone to sell to—and those to whom you try to sell must be both *willing* and *able* to buy. A want or a need is not sufficient. Prospects must have not only the desire, but also the means, whether in cash or credit, to complete the purchase. They should have too an interest that can be sincerely developed, an interest that, when effectively tuned into, will lead them to buy.

Only through the careful locating and qualifying of prospects can you find out who these "live" individuals are— these prospects with both a desire to buy and a capacity to pay (as opposed to *suspects,* individuals about whom you possess so little information that you cannot call them true *prospects*). To make intelligent sales approaches, you must size up and qualify. These qualified prospects provide the lifeline essential to your selling success. Learn this and you will assure yourself of many productive sales. You will be aiming a precision rifle at a pinpointed target.

To assure a continuous stream of "live" prospects, devote a regular amount of time to this effort each day. Provided you have specific criteria in mind for evaluating and qualifying, this effort will save you valuable time. You will then call most always on those who meet the prospect test. What follows should help you to learn how to distinguish between the prospect and the suspect, build a list of prospects, secure and use vital information, plan a daily schedule, and, finally, prepare the reports required in your selling activity.

Prospecting for Customers

To ensure selling to the most promising prospects, every sales professional can profit from effective and continuous use of a prospecting system. Which system you use, however, will depend on what you are selling. The system required to sell machinery or insurance will, of course, differ from that needed by the sales professional who sells a product in consistent demand by regular customers. Insurance sales professionals must turn up most of their own prospects by prospecting in every interview. In contrast, sales professionals for a wholesale concern, calling on their regular customers have a much easier situation.

Numerous systems may be employed to assist your prospecting efforts; each one's success will depend on your initiative, intelligence, and consistency. Proof of your system's effectiveness will be the growing number of live prospects. Only when you have achieved such effectiveness can you make effective use of your valuable selling time. Suggestions that follow should assist you in the selection, development, and maintenance of a qualified list of prospects.

Suggestion 1: Be a Keen Observer

Keen observers can secure many prospects. Newspapers, social meetings, "just looking" at stores, business, manufacturing plants, and club meetings all provide the alert sales professional with many excellent prospect sources. Names can be obtained and arrangements made to call on interested individuals.

Suggestion 2: Tell What You Do

"Toot your own horn" and let people know what it is that you are selling. Too often, sales professionals fail to realize that a number of genuine prospects may be found by merely disseminating information on their selling interest to the very people with whom they deal. These include bankers, builders, suppliers, painters, electricians, doctors, dentists, lawyers, and many others.

Suggestion 3: Create an Endless Chain of Prospects

An almost inexhaustible supply of prospects can be developed by securing additional names from the people on whom you call;

the satisfied customers whom you have already sold can be especially helpful. But whether they have been sold or not, such an effort should be made in every sales interview. What you do is simply this: Ask your prospect for the names of additional people who might be interested in hearing about your product and some background information on them. Used correctly, much time can be saved in prospecting; it can also provide a continuous supply of references. The machinery sales professional asks about other companies that could use similar equipment and who it is within those companies that does the purchasing; investment counselors ask their prospects about others in the community who have funds to invest. In using the endless chain method, make certain that your original source has no objection to your revealing the source of such information.

An additional assist to this technique is the appropriate cultivation of people who have extensive influence in your community—the centers of influence. These are the people who know and are known, whose opinions carry weight, whose recommendations can be most helpful. Whether they purchase from you or not is not essential; what is essential is that they are convinced of your integrity and sincere interest in others. The important business and professional people in your community compose this group. This is how a sales professional might accomplish this objective:

SALES PROFESSIONAL: (just completing a mutual fund sale to an important young executive in a local company): (Prospect's name), you must be acquainted with a number of young and successful executives like yourself who could assist their own financial programs with an appropriate mutual fund. May I take the liberty of asking those that come quickly to your mind?

PROSPECT: Frankly, I know several, but you can well understand I'm hesitant about ever sending anyone to my friends. I'm sure it takes no stretch of the imagination for you to appreciate my feelings.

SALES PROFESSIONAL: Sure, many people feel the same way. They hesitate to recommend a sales professional to their friends.

PROSPECT: That's the problem . . .

SALES PROFESSIONAL: You will agree, however, that you immediately felt you could place more confidence and trust in me because one of your friends had referred me to you. Isn't that true?

PROSPECT: Naturally, I . . .

SALES PROFESSIONAL: That's just it. And you also have my assurance that I'll call on them only once unless they ask me back, and only then because I can really help them as I did you.

PROSPECT: Well, under those conditions, I'll give you so and so's and so and so's names.

SALES PROFESSIONAL: Your help is deeply appreciated, and be assured I will always act in a manner that will merit your continued confidence. By the way, before I do call on them, a little information on their background would be helpful. May I ask . . .

Suggestion 4: Cold Canvassing

Sales professionals sometimes call on people about whom they have no advance knowledge or information. A method widely used by sales professionals who sell office-to-office and business-to-business, cold canvassing can be efficiently employed in the sale of both tangible and intangible services. Used correctly, it yields a certain number of sales from a number of calls. Most firms that rely on this method develop their own ratios between calls and sales for their sales professionals. A variation of this method is the two-call plan: the sales professional's first call is for the purpose of securing attention and developing interest; arrangement is then made for a subsequent appointment in the near future when the full sales presentation may be given. Still another modification is the use of junior sales professionals. Part of the prospecting function can thus be shifted to someone else for the purpose of saving prospecting time. The senior sales professional is "saved" for the actual sales interview. This technique is used by firms that sell, among others things, home-building materials and oil burners.

Suggestion 5: Advertising and Direct Mail

Advertising in such media as newspaper, television, and radio is used to supplement other methods of securing prospects. The inquiries that are secured through the return of coupons or requests for samples are turned over to sales professionals for follow-up.

Direct mail is a great aid in getting you in to see prospects because their interest has already been aroused by letters sent directly to them. It is especially effective with products and services for which there was no previous conscious need. Insurance companies often make use of these letters by inviting the prospect to call the office or to complete and return the enclosed card.

Suggestion 6: The Telephone

With the telephone you have a splendid way to dial your way to sales and also to conserve precious time. Only those individuals are visited who have shown receptiveness to your calls, those who have evidenced an interest in your products or services. Telephone use reduces travel and writing time.

Suggestion 7: Company Activities, Exhibits, and Demonstrations

Every efficiently managed sales department will have maintained careful prospect and customer records. A new person in a territory (in a type of selling situation where regular calls are made) will quickly be able to confirm the status of an account from the records. Often, you will find your sales manager willing to devote time to better acquainting you with prospects, customers, and conditions in your territory. The good relationships between various departments and the sales department will also provide a source of new leads.

Many industries and businesses, among them furniture, machinery, and appliance producers, in which the products are heavy and bulky, use public shows, exhibitions, and demonstrations to attract buyers.

Suggestion 8: Libraries and Lists

You should use your public library to assist in the development of prospect lists. The numerous books, periodicals, newspapers, reports, directories, registration and trade association publications, rating agencies, clippings, speeches, and other materials are excellent sources from which to secure the names of prospects.

Finally, there are the prepared lists of classified prospects of every kind that are sold on a commercial basis. Whether it is the names of lumber dealers or pharmacies that are wanted, these lists will provide the desired information. Available too are telephone, trade, professional, and social directories that are all classified. Also to be considered are the many organization membership lists—service clubs, country clubs, chambers of commerce, advertising, and sales executive clubs—that can be of tremendous value.

About Your Prospects

To raise your selling average, spend time in preliminary investigation to find out as much as possible in advance of your first call about the prospects you have secured and their problems. Find out all you can about prospects' needs for your products or service, their ability to pay, and whether they have the authority to make buying decisions. You will find that advanced knowledge about your customers, their business, and their needs will help you to radiate confidence and enthusiasm. You will have the feeling of being on solid ground and you have a good reason for making the call. Prospects realize that a genuine effort has been made to find out how you can help them solve problems. The following four areas indicate what you should know about your prospect:

1. *Prospect needs and requirements.* The "big little facts," which include spelling and pronouncing your prospects' names, knowing something about their hobbies, sports interests, and educational backgrounds, and the many pieces of information about their personality and individual traits, all contribute to improved reception and rapport between buyer and seller. Company policies established for sales, merchandising supplier relations, and finance all afford important insights into the methods used to conduct business.

   Information about the capital, capacity, and character of your prospects and customers is essential. Nothing is quite so frustrating for sales professionals as their making a sales presentation only to find out the prospect lacks the money to purchase. Just as annoying is the effort to close that reveals that the individual to whom the presentation has been made has no authority to buy. This inability to make the decision may take various forms: sometimes, it involves partners who must be consulted; at other times, several persons in positions of authority must be consulted and interviewed. A good illustration is the case in which a major installation is being considered, and top management and executives in finance, engineering, production, and maintenance may be involved. In still other situations, committees must meet. More will be said about this in the following chapter. Try to see the right person. Ask your prospect if the presentation should be made to others in the firm as well.

2. *Research.* A sales professional's research activities may include everything from careful investigation to indirect inquiry. The account may be one that is important enough to warrant an in-depth survey of key personnel and the methods that have been successfully used in previous sales to them. The advances in science that have produced highly technical and complex machines encourage more and more of such careful research.

3. *Customers, fellow sales professionals, and company.* Interesting facts about prospects may be secured from present customers. Often, they will be willing to supply information about others with similar needs. Tact and good taste plus some careful directed listening will enable you to secure many important and pertinent leads.

   Sales professionals in your own company, sales professionals selling noncompeting lines, even those selling competing lines, can supply you with valuable bits of information. You can expect that a sales professional formerly assigned to your territory will review background on accounts now assigned to you. What is surprising to newcomers in selling is that information can be secured from other sales professionals. The explanation is simple: sales professionals, as do other business people, cultivate friendships with each other. Much information can be obtained in this manner.

   Company correspondence with customers and office records can supply information on order size, purchase frequency, kinds of merchandise preferred, payment record, and other circumstances pertinent to account relationships.

4. *Additional information sources.* Government agencies prepare a wide variety of publications. Reports, pamphlets,
books, and booklets that deal with almost any conceivable
type of marketing problem, sales data, and product information are available to you. State and local agencies also
have much available that can be of real assistance.

Newspapers and chambers of commerce can provide
much pertinent data on business. Newspapers yield information on community interests, personalities, and various
businesses; microfilms on back issues are frequently
available for quick scanning. Information on types of
business, employment situations, area information, and
other pertinent business data are available from chambers
of commerce. Use them.

One final word about information sources: Remember
that prospects enjoy talking about themselves. Try simply
asking them for appropriate information.

Plan! Then Plan Some More

Careful planning hoards time. A well-honed phrase is "Plan your
work and then work your plan." Recognize that time is the most
valuable commodity you have. Planning and maximizing the use
of time assures that essential activities such as prospecting, telephone calls, paperwork, preparation of sales presentations, record
keeping, and follow-up will all be accomplished. You should feel
about time as the Coca-Cola Company feels about thirst: big as
they are, they recognize that any one thirst quenched by something
other than Coca-Cola, whether water or a competing soft drink, is
a "thirst lost forever." So your time should be carefully spent—it
is anything but inexhaustible.

You must prepare a daily schedule of activities based on objectives to be accomplished if you are to build and maintain

an effective selling program. You must define clearly whether your objectives are to be in terms of units sold, dollar sales, gross profit for your company, missionary activities, or other standards. Plans are then set up to accomplish these objectives.

The following three-way plan can be used to accomplish these objectives.

Calls and Interviews with Customers and New Prospects

A current card or computer-generated index on each customer and prospect will help you remember vital information that can increase your opportunity to make sales. From it you should prepare an appointment schedule for your daily calls; from it you should alert yourself to all the special things that have to be done during that week or month. Check to see which regular customers should be visited and make plans to visit a number of prospects whom you have good reason to call on based on careful preprospecting activity. Your plan should be a flexible one so that alternative customers or prospects in the vicinity, where possible, may be visited when, because of unexpected delays or other reasons, it becomes impossible to follow the schedule originally prepared. Some situations will demand that such calls assure your selling as many prospects and customers in a day's time as the type of buyer you call on and the nature of your product or service will allow.

A few more suggestions about this index file: include data on prospects as individuals and appropriate background information about the business or the company they represent. Include in your personal information a note on the correct pronunciation of their names, their addresses, phone numbers, experience, education, interests, and other pertinent information. Additional facts about the company or business including its name, size, location, credit rating, and type of management, should complete the data.

A Time- and Money-Saving Route Plan

Get familiar with the geography of your selling area; careful routing will conserve your time and energy. Travel will be minimized as you strive to make every call the shortest distance between two points. Maps will help you in this plan to go exactly where you want to in the shortest time. Try to avoid the major errors in routing: unnecessary doubling back and territory criss-crossing. Unfortunately, some sales professionals think a change in geography—driving forty miles to the next city or town where the "grass is greener"—is the answer, when extra effort and striving harder would prove the key to more sales in the very city they were scheduled to visit.

An excellent procedure to use for improved routing is this: divide the area you cover into sections for convenient visits, then coordinate these areas and activities into a master plan.

Reports, Telephone, and the Daily Activities Check

Regardless of whether written records are required by your company, be sure to keep them; they can be of tremendous assistance to you. Although each company usually has its own forms, among the basic ones are the daily call report, weekly call summary, monthly activity report, and expense form. The call reports include such information as the purpose of the call, degree of accomplishment, and further actions, if any, to be taken. These various reports also contain data on market conditions, product interest, and the competitive situation. Careful completion of such forms and reports enables you to compare accomplishments with original objectives; in effect, they represent your own achievement record.

Just as you set aside a portion of the day for record keeping, a specific period of time should be set aside to make your phone calls. Earlier, the value of the telephone as a tool for reaching prospects quickly was noted. In the section pertaining to arranging the interview, you will find an excellent illustration of efficient use of the telephone.

The Lifeblood of Selling

Efficient prospecting, as you have seen, is the lifeblood of selling. Successful sales professionals give most careful thought, effort, and attention to efficient prospecting. The future of sales professionals is inextricably bound up with their ability to locate prospects, find out about their background and interests, and then serve them in terms of their own best interests. Once you have prospects and know something about them, you are then ready to secure face-to-face interviews with them.

How to Get All the Prospects You Want

You can take advantage of state-of-the-art technology combined with good old-fashioned telephone sales skills, new discoveries in persuasive communications, and innovative direct mail to get all the good prospecting appointments you want. Let's address how you can have an extra 150 to 250 good prospect meetings over the next twelve months using a comprehensive prospecting system.

State-of-the-art prospecting consists of target market lists, contact management software, introductory letters, a trained telephone prospector, a presentation or script (including answers to objections), follow-up letters, and the ability to monitor and track results. Why is this so important?

To begin with, most people in the sales profession know prospecting is the name of the game. How many times have you heard an associate say, "If I can only get in front of the prospect, I can make the sale"? So, if you need to prospect to succeed, doesn't it make sense to be as good a prospector as possible, or at least have as good a prospecting system as possible? Yet, many sales professionals acknowledge that they don't prospect as well as they'd like. Certainly, they don't make the phone calls they know are needed to be as successful as they'd want to be.

Why don't sales professionals make all the phone calls they should? First of all, no one likes to dial a phone fifteen to twenty times an hour and hear that the prospect you want to speak with is not in, is in a meeting, is otherwise engaged, is not available, or just does not want to speak with you. And if the prospect does agree to take the call, most of the time he or she is not at all interested in continuing a conversation, let alone meeting with you.

A good deal of call reluctance develops as a result of all this inability to get through, compounded with refusals that most sales professionals interpret as rejection. It's understandable that sales professionals would rather occupy themselves with paper-work, calling friends, speaking to peers, or doing all the dozens of things they know they can do rather than get on the telephone and try to get through to a stranger. Therefore, most sales professionals don't make the phone calls that are required to be super successful in this business.

There is also that "hunter-skinner" syndrome. Sales professionals who do some prospecting or receive referrals and find prospects to meet with get involved in working on prospects, developing proposals, and coming back to meet with them several times, as is generally necessary in selling to larger accounts. So, while working on developing your business with existing prospects, you are not making phone calls to identify new prospects to talk with because it is certainly a lot more fun to prepare for interviews with them and go out on those interviews rather than spend a couple of hours on the telephone every day trying to find new prospects to speak with.

Thus, the hunter-skinner syndrome occurs. When you are hunting for new prospects to talk with, you are not skinning; that is, you are not selling. And when you are involved in a selling process, you are not hunting; that is, you are not prospecting.

Therefore, there is a continuous peak-and-valley wave that takes place for sales professionals who have a number of prospects to speak with. While they are on their peak, they either make the sale or do not make the sale, and when they are through, they are in the valley and have to start all over again. These are recurring cycles that keep you at your particular level of earning.

Develop a Program

Fortunately, there is a way to break out of whatever comfort zone you're in. You can smooth out the peaks and valleys and reach a higher plateau. Many of the more successful sales professionals are developing programs that allow them to have a continuous number of new prospects pouring through their funnel of opened accounts. It is recommended that you hire prospectors to continually send out introductory letters, call the new prospects, qualify them, and arrange definite appointments for you to go out and meet with new people. This is an application of the division of labor principle: you delegate telephone prospecting to a telemarketer or telephone solicitor. Perhaps you may already be doing this.

Computer resources are available that you can use to send out your preapproach letters so that when the call is made, it's no longer a cold call but a warm one. After the call takes place, an outcome has occurred: the telemarketer is granted the interview, or there is a "No," a "Call me later," a "Send me information," or some other response. With the aid of modern personal computers and available software, follow-up letters are prepared in advance; they take all these possible outcomes into account, and the appropriate letter is mailed. This sets up the next follow-up call, which will ultimately lead to better relationships and to more and more appointments.

For example, suppose a prospect asks you to call in three weeks, and you not only agree, you also send the prospect a short letter confirming that you'll call. It's going to be difficult to put you off the next time.

You see, the problem has always been that it takes too much time and effort to have an administrative assistant send out all of these follow-up letters. You know it's the right thing to do, but most sales professionals don't have the time or resources to do it. With modern computer software, these problems fall by the wayside. You just push a button and a letter is prepared, and it's all personalized in exactly the way you want it.

Using this system, a good telephone solicitor can, in time, get as many as 40 to 50 percent of the people on a typical list to say yes to a meeting. Now, this is not the first time you call; this is after making a number of calls and sending out a number of letters.

How can you go ahead and do this kind of program yourself? Well, the first step, as in every sound business objective, is to develop a plan. The first question you need to answer is: Who is it that I want to sell to? You also have to set your sights on a new market that you would like to get into. For example, if you have been selling to people at home, plan on now going after small business people. If you have been selling to small business people, plan on approaching businesses that are a little bit larger. In other words, keep doing whatever you've been doing and supplement that by going after another market that has the potential of being more lucrative.

Another planning decision you need to make is whether you are going to use a manual system, which is simply to have a telemarketer cold call into a target list, or use a computer software package in conjunction with your program. You should be using an automated telemarketing system. There are just too many advantages in using software; it's not smart not to use it. There are many good software packages available on the market.

Incidentally, with leasing programs available, it is possible to own an excellent desktop computer system or a notebook computer for a couple of hundred dollars a month, or even less. You can even include a color printer. This will allow you to have effective prospect management, preapproach, and follow-up letters and lead tracking.

Another decision you need to make is whether you should have your own in-house program or use an outside service. Generally, in-house programs work better than outside services. Outside services that make appointments for you may be disappointing; you may find that prospects don't expect you, and when you are expected, they don't have any idea of what you are there to speak to them about. Of course, there are exceptions.

It is usually better to have your own telemarketer, with whom you can communicate so that a relationship develops and the program gets more refined. If, for example, you go to an appointment and you are not speaking to the proper decision maker, come back to your office, and you tell your telemarketer, "Next time you schedule an appointment for me, be sure that you ask if this person can make a decision." It won't take very long for that person to learn and improve.

On the other hand, if you are dealing with a service bureau, there is very little communication with the person or people doing the calling. You take whatever appointments have been set up for you, and many are not going to be satisfactory. However, if you are selling to large groups, a service company can be effective. In most cases, highly successful sales professionals should almost always have their own in-house telemarketer.

Develop a List

Once you have decided what market to pursue and made the decision whether to use your own in-house program or an outside service, the next step is to acquire a list. Many companies are available that can provide you with a list of individual companies in any industry or group of industries with the requisite number of employees and range of financial earnings. For example, besides Dun & Bradstreet, there are American Business Lists and Ponton. For lists of individuals, there are American Consumer Lists and Investor Resources.

Because you are going to use a computer-assisted telemarketing approach, that list is best acquired on a floppy disk as opposed to a hard copy printout. This allows your computer software to utilize the information without having to input it manually. You save many, many hours. It is more expensive to have a list on a floppy disk; however, it is much more cost-effective.

You are also going to want to create a number of preapproach and follow-up letters. The letters should be short, sweet, and simple. Get to the point directly. Short letters are read; longer letters are not always read. Be direct and friendly. The conversational tone is best, rather than a formal one.

What works in direct mail is selling the value of the next contact: a telephone call. It's important not to give too much information, just sell the next step. It is very effective to enclose something tangible in the letter that the prospect can feel, like a novelty or puzzle. This arouses curiosity and improves the "open" rate. Your letter should relate to the enclosed object in some manner. You can also use a color printer to make your letter stand out even more.

One idea is to enclose a chess piece, any piece, even a pawn. You can then write about the missing piece in the prospect's financial strategy. Because chess is synonymous with strategy, enclosing a piece is relevant. Most important, prospects will remember the chess piece a lot better than your letter. They are more likely to take your call when their assistant says, "It's that salesperson who sent you the chess piece." It also is an easy icebreaker. That's just one idea. People are more likely to open a letter that contains a physical object.

When you reach your prospects, you remind them of the letter that contained the novelty item. They very likely will have forgotten the content of the letter, but will remember the novelty and allow you to make a brief phone presentation. Again, this is when you sell only the value of a face-to-face appointment without going into great detail about the specific concepts you'll present.

Develop an Approach

Part of this process is to decide on the approach you will use in both the letters and the phone calls: Is this going to be a general or a specific approach? The general approach talks about the whole subject; the specific approach takes on a segment of it. An example of a typical general approach is one that many sales professionals in the financial services industry have been trained to say: "I have an idea I would like to talk to you about that will allow you to create, preserve, and accumulate wealth in spite of high taxes." Here you are talking about a subject of general interest, using pretax dollars that would ordinarily go to the IRS, but you are not saying how you would specifically use them.

A specific approach is when you take a definite, single product and talk to your prospect about it. For example, "I'd like to tell you about a deferred compensation program that will allow you and some of your key executives to defer income in a manner that will keep your taxes low and help you to accumulate wealth without paying the IRS a premium."

Once you have decided on the approach, test it yourself. Or, of course, you can always have an associate or someone else whom you trust do that, and you can then turn that approach into a presentation. Let's look at scripting. It's suggested that you have a planned, not a canned, presentation. A good presentation is composed of six steps: preparation, approach, probe, presentation, close, and postclose. (Incidentally, although the purpose of this is to give your prospector a track to run on, you can certainly use these principles yourself.)

Preparation

The preparation phase consists of two parts: objective and subjective. The objective part is having all the relevant information in front of you that relates to making a telephone call: your presentation guideline or script, answers to basic questions, answers to major objections, facts about your prospect, everything that relates to the appointment-setting process. This is your right-brain material.

Subjectively, telemarketers and sales professionals can be trained to approach the call as if they already had a successful outcome. They are encouraged to take a few seconds to clear their memory of the last call; then they can visualize the results they want. How would you feel if you picked up the phone, dialed, spoke to someone, and got an appointment? It would feel good, right? Well, feel good going into the call. Feel the way you would feel if you had already gotten the outcome you want and that facilitates your reaching your objective.

Approach

The approach is a statement you make to gain the immediate positive attention of a prospect. Many sales professionals find that the "you/me" approach works best. In this scenario, you talk about the other person first, then tie into you. For example, say to a prospect, "I imagine you're good at running a business and making a profit, and we're good at helping you keep more of the money you earn from your business." If you say something that is true about your prospect, and then say something about yourself, the prospect is more apt to believe you. On the other hand if you talk about yourself first, the prospect is more apt to be skeptical. If the prospect agrees with what you've said about him or her, he or she will tend to agree with your next statement. You first, me second works really well.

Probe

In the probe portion of a presentation, you want to ask some qualifying questions, such as, "Are you married? Do you have a business partner?" Depending on what your objective is, you need to prepare a list of appropriate questions; ideally, there should be only two to four at most. Your questions should do one of two things: qualify the prospect so you know you are talking to someone who can make a decision and can afford your services, and/or help that person recognize that he or she has a need. For example, if you find you are speaking with a person who has a business partner, you could say, "If anything happened to your partner, how would you like to be in business with his or her spouse, or better yet, the spouse's next spouse?"

You next want to present to your prospect some benefits as to why he or she should meet with you. For example (using the financial services industry again), a benefit you might use is, "Because we do assist our clients in keeping their business going in spite of death and disability and you don't have any other program now, it really is to your advantage to see what we have to offer you, isn't it?" Whenever possible, the benefit should relate to what prospects told you about themselves, or what you may have learned about them from another source.

Presentation, Close, and Postclose

The purpose of the presentation section is to create some desire on the part of the prospect to meet with you. If the prospect doesn't have any desire, there is no point in going into the next phase, which is the close. The close is simply asking for an appointment: "I can meet with you for about fifteen minutes next week. How is Tuesday, or is Thursday better?" Of course, it is always advantageous to give an alternative choice: "Are mornings or afternoons better?" Don't just ask for a meeting: give a couple of alternatives. Make it easy for prospects to say yes.

Make it seem as informal as you can. You might say, "I'd like to drop by for twenty minutes to meet you and show you a few new ideas. If I'm there any longer than that, it will only be because you asked me to stay. Fair enough?" Once you've set the appointment, the next part is important to avoid cancellations or other forms of buyers' remorse. You simply put the person in the future, happy with his or her meeting with you. This works in the following way: "And after you see what I have to show you and we discuss it, I know you're going to feel good about our meeting." Leaving the person with an expectation of good feelings in the future is an excellent way to *postclose.*

Everyone knows that most of the time, it's not this easy. More often than not, you receive an objection like "I'm not interested," "I already have a sales professional I'm dealing with," "I'm all taken care of," "I just had it reviewed," and so on. What separates super sales professionals from the others is the ability to overcome prospects' resistance to the meeting. An excellent technique is "I understand and still . . ." It works like this: Whatever the objection, you say, "I understand" and you repeat the objection. For example, "I understand you already have a sales professional you deal with, and still (now you give a benefit). We do specialize in this area as well. It's like giving you a second opinion at no cost."

The key is the phrase "and still" instead of "but." "But" is a red flag: here comes the rebuttal. "And still" is noncombative; it guides the prospect without making him or her defensive.

A variation on this is "I can certainly understand that and still (give benefit)." If you use this technique, you will be favorably surprised at the number of additional appointments you set.

Another possibility that often occurs when attempting to set an appointment is that you are asked a question. You answer it and then you're asked another one and perhaps one more. After you answer, the person you are speaking with says, "Thanks.

You've been very helpful. I'll think about it and get back to you. Good-bye." And you're left there on the other end, feeling used, abused, and abandoned.

This need never happen to you again if you use the "say it/ask it" technique. You are asked a question, you answer it, then you ask one back. For example, a prospect asks, "Just exactly what do you do?" You answer, "I work with companies like yours, analyzing their financial requirements to determine exactly what is needed to maintain the continuity of their business in the event of a problem. Then I assist you in implementing the right solution. When is the last time you saw such an analysis?"

By asking a question after answering one, you regain control of the conversation. The person who asks the last question—not the person who does all the talking—is the one controlling the conversation.

You can also use this technique with the phrase, "If I'm there longer than twenty minutes, it will only be because you asked me to stay. Fair enough?" The first part, "If I'm there longer than twenty minutes, it will only be because you asked me to stay," is the "say it." The "fair enough" is the "ask it."

Now that you have this presentation, you can test it again yourself or you can work with the telemarketer you hire.

Develop a Telemarketer

The next step is to find a telemarketer who is going to be making these calls. An excellent way to get your best people is to place an ad in the local newspaper. One way to select from the best choices is simply to look at the classified section under telemarketers or telephone solicitors and see what the going rate is. Whatever that rate is, whether it is $12/hour or $15 or more depending on your geographic area, place an ad advertising an extra 50¢ to $1.00 an hour. If people are receiving $12/hour, more people will call you for your $12.50/hour ad. This attracts the largest number of people. You will find it worthwhile to pay a little bit more money to get someone who is going to perform rather than to pay a little less money and not get good results.

When people respond to your ad, have a presentation ready that will guide you toward qualifying and then selling them on the appointment. You do want to be sure to have the good people come in to see you. Again, use the same six steps: prepare, approach, probe, present, close, and postclose. Listen for quality of voice, basic intelligence, enunciation, and a positive attitude. Ask yourself: "Is this someone I am enjoying speaking with? Is he or she easy to listen to? Or do I just want to hang up?" However you answer these questions, chances are that your prospects will feel the same way.

Says one MDRT sales professional: "Once, I had a totally inexperienced telemarketer who had a beautiful resonant baritone voice that was very, very pleasant to listen to. Even though he had no experience, he was willing to be trained and turned out to be super on the phone. People enjoyed talking to him. They liked the sound of his voice and agreed to appointments."

As much as possible, restrain your desire to meet with your applicants face-to-face. Conduct your interview by telephone. How directly will he or she answer your questions? Is he or she positive? Whatever questions you can ask in person, you can ask by telephone. And primarily, do not, as a rule, be interested in the specific answer so much as in the way the person sounds. Remember, you're looking for someone who is capable of setting appointments. That person does not have to sell the program; that is your job.

Once you have selected three or four people who sound like they can do the job, have them come in to make sure they feel comfortable in your office environment. Sometimes, you find that people who sound very good are somewhat disappointing in their personal appearance. But don't let this sway your hiring decisions.

As a rule, you will find it much more effective to have people work from your office. To confirm your hiring decision, you can also use tests such as the Personal Sales Profile. It identifies four behaviors: assertiveness, influencing, steadiness, and detail consciousness. These tests can be obtained through bookstores or through various specialty vendors. The Personal Sales Profile is available in the MDRT *How-To Book: A Practice Management Guide.*

Step Up to the Plate

To get the appointment, to open the door, to get a chance at bat, you don't have to sell the whole ball of wax. You simply have to appeal to your prospect. Says another MDRT sales professional:

> One of the best telephone prospectors I ever met was a man named Chuck. Chuck had a rather unprepossessing appearance. However, he had a beautiful, mellifluous voice and genuinely liked people, especially administrative assistants. And he was quite adept at getting through to executives by chatting with their assistants, exchanging pleasantries, saying things like, "Boy, you sound good for a Wednesday morning. Did you find some money?" And after a few comments like these, he would say, "By the way, is your boss in?" And he would be quickly connected to the executive—sometimes, people on the level of the chairman of the board at Boeing, for example.
>
> After getting through to the executive, he would say, "Boy, you're tougher to reach than a senator in Europe," which would invariably evoke a chuckle. He would follow that with, "You know, I found out how you can take it all with you." And the executive would say, "Really, how?" And Chuck would answer, "Bank of America has branches all over hell." It didn't take him long to develop excellent rapport with the executive and he'd set an appointment.
>
> When Chuck's boss (the sales professional who hired him) would come to see the executive, the prospect would be

disappointed that Chuck wasn't along and would say something like, "I hope you know as much about it as Chuck." Chuck, of course, knew virtually nothing about the program. He simply was setting the appointment. And the sales professional at this point, would say, "Well, I think I do. By the way, what did Chuck tell you?" Most of the time, the answer would be something like, "Well, I don't really remember, but it did sound very interesting." It's more important to be a people person to get the appointment than to know a great deal about what the product is all about.

One of the key factors in a successful telephone appointment-setting program is to provide training to your telephone solicitor. It isn't necessary for the telemarketer to know your business that well, but in time he or she will learn more and more about it. However, it is vital that the telemarketer learn as many techniques and skills as possible that will allow him or her to keep getting appointments. There's a great deal of training material available in every company and there are certainly a lot of cassettes on telephone techniques that are available for purchase.

In the past, one of the ways to ensure that your telemarketer was on track was to have him or her check a report sheet on a daily basis. Now, contact-management software automatically keeps track of activity and produces reports. This means telemarketers can spend more time on the phone, where they can do the most good.

The bottom line is that telephone calls and letters, used in conjunction with each other, have a powerful synergistic effect in creating relationships. After all, you must have a relationship with a prospect to turn him or her into a client.

Several alternatives are available. Starting at the bottom, the least effective way is to simply make a phone call to a targeted market to set an appointment. If you have a very, very strong telemarketer, this will work just as some of you can pick up a telephone, call people you don't know, and get appointments with them. Those who are very good on the telephone can do that.

Another variation on this approach is to call someone and ask for permission to send a letter or other information that would relate to some problems you know would be of interest to them. You are calling first, and asking for permission to mail and follow-up.

A third approach, and this one depends on your having a good list by which you know the correct name of the decision maker, is to send a letter to your prospect and then follow up by calling that prospect to arrange a meeting. This is the most effective use of phone and mail.

It is true that there will always be some prospects who will not read your letters. However, if you do have a consistent program and you are mailing letters regularly that are managed by a computer, as discussed below, you will quickly see that you are received much more positively than if you are simply making a cold call.

The system works like this: Every week, your prospector prepares introductory letters to fifty new prospects. Ideally, your letter should contain something that your prospect can feel through the envelope. This arouses curiosity and the letter gets opened. The next week, the telemarketer receives a report that it is time to call those people who have already received letters, or their names appear on the computer screen. When he or she makes the call, it is no longer a cold call, it is a warm call. Many remember the letter, or at least the object that the letter contained.

When you or your prospector follow up with a phone call to request an appointment, you are beginning to create a relationship. If the prospect says yes, a confirmation letter is sent out by the system confirming the date and time of the appointment. If the prospect says no, an "I'm sorry you said no" letter is sent out by the system. If the prospect says, "Later," you send a letter saying, "I'll get back to you in two weeks (or whatever), as you suggested." If the prospect says, "Send information," you send information and call him or her again in a week.

Each of these letters leads to the next consecutive event in the system. The confirmation letter for appointments leads to an appointment report that the sales professional takes back to the office and then checks off the outcome: "Got the sale," "Did a fact-finder," "Made the next appointment." Whatever takes place, check off the box and send the next letter in the sequence.

This combination of continuous communication through letters, phone calls, and visits will result in more sales. Can you see how that would work? All those nonappointment outcomes turn into letters that again will trigger phone calls at the appropriate intervals. Sales professionals who have used this system have increased their earnings by 40 percent or more. If you see just three more prospects each week, that's an additional 150 each year. You will surely sell some of them, won't you?

This system allows you to develop a relationship by phone and letter with a large number of people, so that when you finally do get to see them, you're not a stranger. And isn't that what you want?

The Magic of Introductions

The thrill and excitement of making the sale: you would agree that there isn't anything on a business level that can ever replace that excitement.

However, to consistently feel the excitement, you have got to work hard and become an expert in a few key result areas. So goes the saying, "Success is about doing a few key things well—on a consistent basis." This is not a new idea.

The formula for success is already thousands of years old. Aristotle, who lived over three hundred years before Christ, once said, "We are what we repeatedly do. Excellence, then, is not an act but a habit."

In other words, success is about doing a few key things well on a weekly basis, on a regular basis, on a consistent basis—like prospecting. If you want to continuously feel the thrill and excitement of making the sale, then obtaining a continuous flow of high-quality referrals or introductions is vital. An introduction is where you have been so strongly recommended to prospects that they are "presold" in having a meeting with you—even before you have contacted them.

Obtaining these introductions, as opposed to referrals, makes your job even easier because, when you lift the telephone, you are guaranteed an appointment every time.

Perhaps you are already an expert at obtaining referred leads and many of these referrals have helped you achieve moderate success in selling. How do you turn those referrals into introductions?

The secret lies in understanding why many people refuse to give you referred leads in the first place. The main reason why you sometimes fail to get referrals from some of your prospects or clients is that they are afraid of upsetting their friends by sending you to their door. The basic fear at the back of their minds is that their friends may be upset because you have telephoned them, pestering them to buy your service or product.

So, what you do is preempt the objection in the first place. And it's dead easy! All you do is ask for referrals in your normal way (don't change what you're doing already). Simply add the sentence, "Would you mind speaking to them first?" That's the key phrase. Then say, "I won't speak to any of your recommendations until you have had a chance to speak to them first. Is that fair?" And they usually say, "Yes, that's fair enough." What you've done is to remove the hidden objection. Now your prospect or client knows you won't upset his or her friends.

You then phone your prospect or client the following week and say, "Hi, remember those names you gave me? Have you spoken to any of them yet?" The odds are they haven't been phoned yet. So you phone the prospect or client the following week to check again. What you'll probably hear is, "I've spoken to four of them, but only two want to see you."

Now, this might be a longer process than you are used to, but the quality of prospects is brilliant! You then phone the prospect and say, "Hi, it's (your name) here. (Referrer's name) asked me to call you, and said you were interested in talking to me. When can we meet?"

Try this as a telephone approach, and you're guaranteed an appointment because you have been presold by the person introducing you. The key sentence is "I promise I won't contact your recommendations until you have spoken to them first. Is that fair?"

Give this method a try. You will find that if you turn these referrals into introductions, rejection becomes a thing of the past. Now let's move on.

As you probably know, there aren't many new sales ideas. Often, you will find the old ones are still the best ones. If you want to disturb prospects and get them to agree with a need, it usually happens by asking some key questions; for instance, "Why did you buy it before?"

When you are completing a fact-find, you will invariably find out that prospects have purchased products or services similar to the ones that you are offering. The question "Why did you buy it?" will take you straight to their "hot buttons."

They may reply, "Because it was a perfect fit at the time." And you may counter with, "And is that still your main priority?" If they say, "Yes, I suppose so," then you simply establish the level of shortfall and sell your products or services.

On the other hand, if their priorities have changed, you have found out this important fact at an early stage of the sales process and you move on to discuss their other needs. Either way you win—all by asking the simple question "Why did you buy it?"

The Nonverbals of Prospecting

From the moment a prospect sets eyes on you, judgments are being made. You might not have said a word, not one single word, and yet judgments about you are being made. What judgments are being made, consciously or unconsciously, and what are the bases of these and subsequent judgments?

In the first minute of initial contact with another individual, judgments are made about the individual's appearance. Specifically, judgments are being made about body build, figure, attractiveness, and dress. In an era of physical fitness, one's body is an indication of concern for one's own appearance and health, self-management, and self-control.

Simply put, if you can't manage yourself, how can you manage others? Being out of shape, heavy, or just plain fat is perceived as more than a health risk; it is a professional liability.

Research is very clear about the importance of physical attractiveness. The attractive individual is more likely to get the job than the unattractive individual. Consciously or unconsciously, we initiate conversations with and seek out the attractive person rather than the unattractive person.

As an example, a cosmetic company tells their trainers how important makeup is in enhancing certain features, particularly the eyes. They report that facial features are critical in the first forty-five seconds. Although we think about aroma only slightly, aroma does make a difference. We associate aroma with food both positively and negatively. Real estate agents recommend baking bread when a prospective buyer is inspecting your home. In terms of perfume or aftershave, a gentle, positive fragrance enhances the first impression, particularly if the individual identifies the fragrance with an expensive perfume rather than a cheap cologne. On the other hand, one might be turned off by the smell of alcohol, cigarettes, or "smelly cigars." In one case, the turnoff is subconscious; but quite often in a health conscious society, the turnoff is at a very conscious level.

Over the years, we have been bombarded by articles, books, and seminars on dressing for success. Clothing is an index to your personality. People make judgments about you from the clothes you wear in terms of style and color. Of the two genders, women are more observant and more critical about clothing than men. And more than to please men, women dress to please other women.

In one critical minute, you have made an impression. Hopefully, that first impression is a positive one that will help set the tone for the conversation and a successful communication. But what about beyond that first minute? What is important? What makes the critical difference between success and failure?

One critical element is eye contact. When you fail to establish eye contact, your prospects feel there is less interaction, less personalization, less interest in them as individuals. Prospects may ask, "Are you communicating with me or are you talking at me?" When you fail to achieve eye contact, prospects feel you are not listening. Be an active listener and establish good eye contact.

Staring at prospects or giving what might be called the "elevator look," will make them feel uncomfortable. It's human nature to like an individual to look, but we don't like an individual to stare. Eye contact is influenced by several factors. First, the closer you are to another individual, the more you are aware of the eyes. For example, if you want to confront your prospects, you would invade their space, change your posture, make one of several gestures, and stare. If you blink a lot, the other individual will feel you're weak or hesitant to carry out your threat. But if you lock your eyes directly into your prospect's eyes with a strong stare, there will be little doubt as to your intent.

When you're farther away from prospects, they don't feel you are staring. They will be comfortable in the situation and thus comfortable with you. A second factor that influences eye contact is power. An individual with less power is required to maintain eye contact.

Another factor that many people tend to forget is height and body type. Perhaps you think of power as it relates to status; you would be absolutely correct. Eye contact and status are definitely related. But power is also perceived in terms of control, of who is in control of the interaction. Two tall people are equal, but a tall person and a small person are not.

Back in 1988, after the presidential debate between Michael Dukakis and George Bush, Dukakis went over to George Bush to shake hands. Dukakis, who is much shorter than Bush, seemed dwarfed by the "powerful" Bush. If you are taller than the other individual, allow more space between you. Also, move more quickly to a seat. This will minimize height and help relax the other individual.

However, there are those who are well aware of the advantages of height and go out of their way to emphasize it. J. Edgar Hoover, legendary director of the FBI, would greet new agents by standing on a pedestal and shaking hands with them. Senator John Tower of Texas, who was short, had a special long desk made for him to give him more power, and he had his chair on a riser to give him added height.

The size of the pupil is influenced by light, but is also influenced, subconsciously, by one's attitude. When an individual is startled or shocked, his or her pupil size will become larger. Eye contact is of critical importance in face-to-face communication. Of the two genders, women are more eye-oriented than are men.

Another important area of nonverbal communication is facial expressions. Facial expressions can say volumes. Researchers have found the most universal form of communicating emotions is through facial expressions.

One area of nonverbal communication or body language is proxemics, the study of space. Unlike Captain Kirk and the crew of the *Enterprise,* we're talking about the space between individuals:

physical and psychological. A group of individuals on stage allow themselves a certain amount of space between each other, but if they were in an elevator, the dimensions of space would change.

If you want to relax prospects, you need to be aware of the psychological reaction to space. There are several factors to consider. The first is relationship. Researchers have clearly shown that we place ourselves closer to people we like than to those we dislike or are uncomfortable with. With new prospects, when the relationship is not established, keep to the eighteen-inch bubble. This is particularly true when dealing with executives or individuals of high status; they require and expect greater space and distance. When you invade their territory, you create more than discomfort; you imply a feeling of disregard of the individual's position. The person in authority should change the space dimension, not you. If you change the space, you are perceived as being aggressive and perhaps disrespectful.

Too often, men make the mistake of changing space with women they perceive as attractive; consequently, the woman pulls back and becomes psychologically uncomfortable. If a woman invades the territory, she is perceived as being too aggressive.

We have a tendency to allow less distance to older people. Yet, their perception of space and distance is no different from that of younger people. If there are exceptions to the eighteen-inch bubble other than relationship, it is age and culture. With very small children, we allow a lot less space and we allow touching. Some cultures, for example, Arabs and Israelis, require less distance.

When prospects are comfortable with you, there will be direct eye contact and less distance. Prospects will perhaps lean forward and might even nod in agreement. When prospects are uncomfortable with you, there will be greater distance, indirect eye contact, pupil size may increase, and they may even turn their bodies away from you, cross their legs or arms, dip their shoulders away from you, or take other evasive action.

If prospects start to fidget, you are losing their attention. Sometimes, prospects will play with a coffee cup, pen, or paper clip, or perhaps move papers. If this occurs, you need to change the topic or your delivery. However, it isn't always your prospects who are fidgeting. It may be you.

Ralph Waldo Emerson wrote, "What you do speaks so loud that I cannot hear what you say." Quite often, we give two conflicting messages: the verbal message says one thing and the nonverbal message another. When prospects are given a double-edged message, they believe the nonverbal over the verbal. They believe the nonverbal is the unconscious indicator of true feelings and intent, and they perceive the verbal as a conscious attempt to deceive or to hide one's true motives.

Another important area in nonverbal communication is gestures. Generally, we think of gestures with public speaking, but what about gestures one-on-one? Strong gestures connote power and self-confidence; weak gestures connote weakness and low self-esteem. Be careful: you can overpower your prospects with gestures that are too strong.

Don't overgesture. If you do, the gestures will lose their value as a means of emphasis and will become distracting. The other individual will pay more attention to your gestures than your words. Be very careful of your fingers. The thumb counts in German cultures as one, the second finger can be strength and yet parental, the third finger gets you into trouble, the fourth finger is physically difficult to use, and the pinkie a sign of weakness. The back of the hand in some cultures is perceived as an insult.

Before moving to the area of touch, let's spend a minute discussing legs. Ordinarily, you might not think twice about a man crossing his legs. It is comfortable and usually accepted in Western culture. But it is an insult to Orientals and at times is perceived in Western cultures as creating a barrier or a wall. If prospects cross their legs in a conversation, you generally can perceive this in the same way as if they crossed their arms: they are uncomfortable, uneasy, or just plain defensive. If prospects wiggle their legs, they are generally becoming bored. If they do this in the early portion of the conversation, they may be bored as well as not very comfortable.

Watch yourself! You may also be giving cues of boredom and discomfort. This is particularly true when listening.

Americans are touchy about tactile communication. Change the context, and you change the warrant or justification for touching. In our culture, a man will allow a male friend to put an arm around his back and touch his shoulder. But if he is not a friend, the gesture makes men uncomfortable. Even if he is a friend, the touch is brief. It is generally perceived as patronizing or insulting when a man touches a woman who is not his friend; if a woman touches a man who is not her friend, the familiarity is perceived as being overly aggressive.

The handshake, as you well know, is critical as a greeting, but is forgotten as a means of congratulating prospects for making a good decision. You may remember the handshake when prospects say yes to purchasing your products, but forget the importance of the handshake when they say "Let me think about it."

Too often, we think of body language only in terms of the individual cues: eyes, space, gestures, and touch. We sometimes forget to think of body language as a series of cues. If you hold someone's hand and change the space and then the eye contact, you will notice the difference in reaction.

When all is said and done, 92 percent of initial face-to-face communication is nonverbal and only 8 percent is verbal. We watch our words; isn't it time we watched our body language?

Chapter 3

Prospecting with the Telephone

A salesperson's best friend is the telephone, but the telephone can be an enemy, too—at once a connection to the prospect as well as a barrier between the two of you. Success with the telephone takes skill, discipline, and perseverance. Let's examine some techniques, including phone scheduling and phone tracking, for successfully turning the telephone into a salesperson's best sales tool.

A Dozen Ways to Make Cold Calling Fun

Call reluctance doesn't exist because sales associates *don't know* what to do on phone calls. It exists because people don't want to do what they know. It's time to stop dealing with the *how to* and start concentrating on the *want to.*

Consider the law of effect that, loosely translated, says we continue to do the things that make us feel happy and don't do those things that make us feel neutral or unhappy. Conclusion: If we *have to,* let's make sure we *want to.* Following are twelve ways to enjoy cold calling.

1. Dress for comfort.

Forget the old saying "Look good, because how you look will carry over the phone through the tone of your voice." Baloney—dress comfortably. Wear that old silly hat, Chicago White Sox sweatshirt, sweatpants, and all-purpose athletic shoes (laces open). Here's important news: The prospect cannot see you! You control your tone of voice, and when you are dressed comfortably, it is often easier to project a comfortable, relaxed sound. Isn't reducing tension (both yours and the prospect's) your first objective?

2. Change your environment.

Get out of the office. If you don't have a high-quality portable phone, get one. Go home and take your phone out in the back yard, on the deck, wherever you feel the most relaxed. If that would be too great a test for your self-discipline, form an MLC (Misery Loves Company) group and have a group calling session. Sometimes, being with others and using the natural human elements of competition and fear of rejection will spur you on to even greater heights.

3. Know what you want.

Be 100 percent sure you understand the objective of your call, are comfortable with it, believe in it, and are able to articulate that objective. Do you want the prospect to buy right then? To accept your material? To meet with you? What do you want?

Have a detailed plan for all contingencies. What will you say if:

- ✓ Your prospect answers? (You only have a few seconds to capture interest.)

- ✓ You are asked to leave a message on a machine/voice mail? (The message should be designed to intrigue your prospects enough to call you back or to receive your next call.)

- ✓ You must leave a message with another person? (An administrative assistant or family member can write only so much on those little pads.)

4. Set a goal that is acceptable to you.

Perhaps your company requires twenty cold calls, but because that is too many for you, you don't make any. Isn't it better to set your own goal of five and make them?

5. Reward yourself for making your goal.

Knock off early—take a hike, watch some TV in the afternoon, read a "no-brainer" book, go to a movie. Treat yourself to some R&R for your efforts.

6. Keep ratios in mind.

Remember, most sales are made as a result of the effective playing of the number's game. The more people who are aware of your product or service, the better chance you have to make a sale. How many people can you make aware? How many calls do you have to make, on average, before you make a sale? Count the calls you make. It is fun to watch them add up. Share the ever-increasing total with whoever might care.

7. Learn from each call.

Call number one lasted ten seconds before rejection. Call number two lasted fifteen seconds. What did you do differently on the second call to get that extra five seconds?

8. Consider the people you are talking to as peers and equals.

If you feel you are better than they are and you have taken time out of your busy schedule to give them the benefit of your wisdom, you may come across as condescending. If you feel they are better than you and you don't have any position playing in their ball game, you may come across as apologetic.

9. Be excited about your products and services.

If you genuinely believe that what you have to offer your prospects will be of mutual benefit, you should let as many people as possible know about it. Sell yourself first.

10. Take the time for brief notes.

Document on paper or in your computer the important points made in the telephone call to ensure that you will remember them. But watch that you don't overdo it to get out of making the next call: stay on a roll.

11. Conduct an objective reality check.

What is the worst that a prospect can do to you over the telephone? What's the probability of that happening? If the worst happened, what would you do? What is the best that can happen to you during that cold call? Is the best worth risking the worst?

12. Lighten up.

Don't take yourself too seriously. After all, it's not brain surgery. How important is any one call? If they turn you down, you are no worse off than you were before you made the call!

Cold calling, like other elements of the sales process, is an internal and an external game. If you can dial a telephone, and have a reasonable knowledge of and passion for your product or service, you can do the external game of cold calling. But without the inner commitment, without the activity feeling good, you might as well turn your telephone into a planter.

Analyze your pros and cons concerning cold calling and do what you can to increase the pros and negate the cons.

The Telephone: Your Best Sales Tool

Some sales professionals don't believe in doing any prospecting—for them it takes too much time and effort. Instead, they let others do their prospecting for them. You think this sounds preposterous? These observations from one highly successful MDRT associate suggest that your prospecting efforts can be replaced or supplemented by hiring a good telemarketer.

"When you think of it, a typical sales professional's time breakdown is:

✓ 20 percent office work.

✓ 20 percent traveling to appointments.

✓ 40 percent prospecting.

✓ 20 percent sales.

"It seems wrong to spend only 20 percent of the time selling. Although it's obvious that we can't sell without prospecting, we must remember that the only time we are actually making money is when we are selling; so this 20 percent of our time is carrying our whole operation. It's also obvious that if we can cut down the time spent on prospecting, we can spend more profitable time in front of clients or potential clients selling, selling, selling! A third obvious fact is that help is needed to do this. Help of this kind costs money, and for 13 years I've employed two part-time assistants who each work two four-hour shifts a week. That's 16 hours a week. Their sole job is to phone prospects and to make appointments for me. They contact about eight people an hour, or 130 per week. Who do they phone? I give them lists of people. Some can be completely cold; for example, newspaper lists, company magazines, trade journals. Others come from accountants, brokers, and real estate sales offices. The very best of all come from my own client files. I make appointments personally when a client phones me, or when I need to contact a client for any reason. Otherwise, I do almost no prospecting at all."

Do you want to go this way?

"There are many individuals with previous experience in business who would jump at the chance of a few hours work each week. Keeping their minds sharp and active and being involved in an interesting and productive activity away from the domestic routine is far more important to them than the money they earn.

But, of course, both must be satisfying. Some people are widely experienced in customer contact or telephone work already.

"You can get a selection of applicants with a simple advertisement or, better yet, get a headhunter to get them for you. This is faster and you don't use so much of your time interviewing. Put four applicants on trial for a week. Select two applicants for the next week. If one or both fail, you still have two to call on for week three. You will find it is not easy. You could go through 10 or even 20 applicants, and it could take weeks.

"Keep going until you find that pearl without price, someone who enjoys the work and is good at it, someone who will not collapse under the constant rejection, as happens to many. Cherish this person! Do not allow him or her to work too long or they will burn out! I find that four hours a day and no more than three days a week give optimum performance and results.

"When you've found the first one, go out and find a matching pearl as backup. Do not expect your canvasser to be able to make five appointments a day. Remember that he or she will be exactly the same as we all were when we had just started in the business. This person will need to train in the telephone technique just as you were trained. You will need to invest your time in that training.

"I give this person a telephone sales track and insist that it be used exactly as written. For the first two weeks, I start each working day with my new telemarketer. I make the first five telephone calls using the track exactly as I want it to be used. This shows the way, particularly if I succeed in making an appointment. Then I monitor his or her first five calls of the day. We discuss each one before moving on to the next call.

"At the end of the four-hour session, I check the results. We discuss the variation of responses received so that he or she will understand and believe that everyone who uses the telephone for marketing gets the same answers and objections. I show that all objections can be classified as one of the four: *no need, no money, no hurry, no confidence,* and that one of these answers will apply to anything anyone can say. It takes about three weeks for my new employee to settle into the work properly and to become comfortable with the sales track.

"My part does not end here. Supervision is essential. Regular checks are made to see that he or she stays exactly on the sales track. No matter how long this employee works for me, I check regularly. For example, my two assistants have been with me for more than three years, and I still listen in every week or two. Particularly in the early months, most new employees will try to improve the sales track, or to make it nicer or sweeter.

"I can always tell when this is happening because the ratio of appointments to calls declines. I insist, 'You are selling the idea of an appointment to buy. Selling is an exact science. You cannot ad lib in a sale, so you must stay on the sales track.' At first, the new hire will make no effort to qualify the prospects. Making appointments is the first skill for your telemarketer to learn. Qualifying techniques are brought in during week three. The simplest qualifying question we use and one of the most effective is: 'If you really like the product my boss shows you, if it's the best you've seen, how much can you afford per month to purchase it on a payment plan?' Does that sound familiar? There's really nothing new in the world, is there?

"Until week three and beyond, until the new hire really learns to use that phrase, you can personally confirm each appointment the day before and do a little qualifying and weeding out for yourself at the same time. Then discuss with your telemarketer why you cancelled one or two.

"My approximate time split-up now is:

✓ Prospecting (names, client selection, etc.): 15 percent

✓ Appointment making: 5 percent

✓ Office work: 20 percent

✓ Traveling time:	20 percent
✓ Sales time:	40 percent

"My bottom line has improved and continues to improve, because my canvassers are continually working toward more office appointments to reduce travel time, so I get close to 50 percent of my time as selling time. After each sale, I arrange the next interview with the prospect. I ask, 'Will we revisit before or after the end of the year?' or whatever is appropriate. The canvassers enter these appointments into a card follow-up system.

"Quite often, I hear from sales professionals about the difficulty of properly servicing their existing client base as they grow in their industry. My two helpers take away a large part of this strain and at the same time provide me the opportunity to make extra sales.

"I have approximately 500 clients (defined as a customer who hasn't bought in three years, who may not have bought anything for 15 years) and about 650 active clients (defined as a customer who has bought more than once or whose last purchase was within the last three years). If no new business is done within five years, that customer is dropped from the follow-up system. This results in 500 clients, plus 650 clients, for a total of 1,150 on the active list.

"My helpers automatically call everyone on the list at least once a year with the objective of obtaining another sales appointment. If some other problem arises, they refer it to my personal assistant, who can handle 90 percent of them.

"My weekly breakdown of appointments is like this:

Average weekly appointments made:	14

✓ Client service interviews:	2
✓ Client 'second' sales interview:	2

✓ 'Cold call' second sales interview: 1

✓ 'First' sales interview—clients: 6

✓ Less cancellations and postponements: 2

✓ 'First' sales interviews—cold calls: 3

Average weekly appointments completed: 12

"Four out of 10 sales interviews are still from cold calls! I work 40 weeks of the year and the canvassers work 42. The approximate weekly breakdown of their calls must include about 30 calls to the client list so that everyone on the list is contacted annually. Of the 130 calls per week, about 100 are for new appointments, 20 are for sales follow-up, and 10 are for miscellaneous service. My income increases by more than the inflation rate, so I'm going ahead, not backwards. I don't think I could do that without the telephone and two wonderful canvassers who enjoy their work.

"A few words of warning:

1. *Do not* employ your spouse, or a relative, or a friend, or a friend's spouse or relative. Keep this position at the impersonal business level. Could you fire your spouse or your friend's spouse if he or she doesn't or can't produce the results?

2. Some time ago, I bought an automatic telephone canvassing machine and found I was not permitted to use it in my area. Learn the lesson from my experience. Everyone should check local regulations regarding computerized or personal approach telephone marketing before they start."

Chapter 4

Building Networks and Getting Referrals

B y far, the best prospects come from a sales professional's present customers. These referrals are simply prequalified names of potential customers that are secured from other people—people known on favorable basis, such as clients, friends and family, and other centers of influence. The power of referrals is that they are more likely to buy than are other types of prospects. What follows are ideas for networking and generating a multitude of quality referrals—the seeds of a salesperson's success.

The Art of Networking

One of your biggest challenges as a sales professional is the continual development of new, qualified prospects. In reaching higher levels of production, you develop a loyal, referral-based clientele. While these clients and their referrals keep you busy, the key to success is to continually prospect and find new sources of business. The challenge then is how to accomplish this goal while making the best use of your valuable time. Networking is a viable solution.

Let's begin by looking at one particular aspect of networking: how to go from initial contact to a continual flow of referrals, without spending much time or money in accomplishing this objective. First, though, let's clarify the term *networking,* as it is often misunderstood by sales professionals. We are not talking about the stereotypical slick, fast-talking salesperson-type, working the crowd, seeing who's there to con, shaking hands, glad-handing, back-slapping, and saying such clever things as, "Hey, let's do lunch." We're talking about *the cultivating of mutually beneficial, give-and-take, win-win relationships.* Now, make no mistake about it. When implemented correctly, following the road map, and most important, genuinely caring about the other person and his or her needs, these following techniques will absolutely and dramatically increase your referral business.

Let's break the art of networking into three categories: finding prospects, meeting them, and then winning them over and turning them into your "personal walking ambassadors." Before beginning, let's review some of the basics of networking because reviewing basics is so vitally important. Perhaps being reminded of the Hall of Fame football coach Vince Lombardi is a good start. Lombardi led the Green Bay Packers of the 1960s to three world championships and is arguably the greatest coach of all time. Each year on the first day of spring practice, he'd stand before the members of his team—the greatest players of the game. These men were regarded with awe and fear by their opponents because of their incredible skill and prowess. The first thing Coach Lombardi would do on opening day of practice was to stand in front of his team, holding a football in his hand, and say, "Gentlemen, this is a football." Talk about basics!

There are analogies to this story in every sport, but you should understand the value of fundamentals and be open to continually reviewing the basics. Let's quickly do that now and begin with the golden rule of networking: All things being equal, people will do business with, and refer business to, those people they know, like, and trust. An example of this maxim is this story conveyed by a highly successful MDRT sales professional: "I had been using the same dry cleaners for a while. Slowly, over time, they started to consistently do a lousy job, and then almost ruined three suits. The fact that I knew, liked, and trusted them as people no longer came into play. Their quality was not equal; thus, I changed dry cleaners. Had their performance been equal, or even close to equal, they would to this day get my business and referrals. But it wasn't, so they don't."

As long as the products you represent and the service you give are at least equal to the competition's, then it's the "know you, like you, and trust you" factor that will put you over the top. Let's look quickly at the saying, "It isn't what you know, but who you know." That's only partly true. Perhaps you should add just a bit to that saying: "It isn't just what you know, or who you know. It's actually who you know who knows what you do for a living, and when you know that person or someone that person knows needs your products and services." Yes, that is a mouthful, yet there's actually even one more phrase that is necessary to bring it all home: "Providing that first person knows you, likes you, and trusts you." That's where effective personal positioning comes in (to be discussed later).

Next, let's talk about sphere of influence. You should know what that is: the people you know. You have two different spheres of influence, the one you come by naturally and the one you create. Your natural sphere of influence could include immediate family, distant relatives, close friends, and sometimes acquaintances: the person who delivers your mail, the plumber, the tailor, the person who cuts your hair, anyone with whom you come into contact.

The sphere of influence you create is the one that will generate productive activity and keep your referral business on overdrive. Here's why: It's been documented many times, most notably in the book, *How to Sell Anything to Anybody* by Joe Girard, that the average person has a natural sphere of influence of about 250 people. Let's figure that every time you meet someone new, you can assume that person knows about 250 additional people. So take that one step further. Every time you meet someone new (and you are able to establish and cultivate a mutually beneficial, give-and-take relationship, to the point where that person feels as though he or she knows you, likes you, and trusts you), you have just increased your personal sphere of influence by about 250 people. Do that with enough new people and you will develop an enormous, extraordinary personal sphere of influence.

Before detailing the mechanics of networking, let's share one MDRT sales professional's thoughts about something that is often associated with networking, which, in reality, has actually very little to do with it—and that's business cards:

> Business cards are often thought of as a valuable networking tool by those who don't really know better. We've all seen the person who goes around handing out business cards to everyone they see. The inexperienced networkers-to-be watch in amazement as "that guy really works the room." I disagree. I believe that has nothing to do with effective positioning and profitable networking.
>
> Now don't get me wrong, I'm not saying that business cards don't have any benefits; just not the way you might think. Let me very quickly address a couple of benefits of business cards. The first benefit of business cards is that you can win a free lunch at a local restaurant by dropping your business card into a fish bowl. Have you ever done that and actually won a free lunch? Great! If you have, you've paid for your business cards with that one. Of course, that doesn't exactly qualify as networking, does it?
>
> The second benefit of business cards is the one true benefit—and that is, you can use a business card to get the other person's business card. That's fine as long as you realize that your business card, itself, is not going to be responsible for bringing in business.

Now back to networking. When and where can you appropriately network? The answer is practically anywhere and anytime.

Everyday, networking situations arise, from the Chamber of Commerce exchange functions to the racquetball court, PTA meetings, health clubs, airplanes, cocktail parties, one-on-one introductions, and small or large group settings. And networking is almost always appropriate, so long as you don't come across to the other person as though you are "networking" in the stereotypical sense of the word.

Let's use the example of the typical Chamber of Commerce card exchange. Do you belong to your local Chamber of Commerce? If your company doesn't, then buy an associate membership for yourself. The financial investment is minor compared to the business you'll do if—and only if—you know how to cultivate it correctly. The following techniques are applicable in any situation where you'll network from now on. This just happens to be one situation where you can meet a bunch of new networking prospects.

Throughout North America, the Chambers of Commerce have instituted monthly events known as Business before Hours, Business after Hours, Networking Functions, or Card Exchanges. Usually, these events are useless businesswise, although they certainly don't have to be. Regardless of what they're called, the concept is that Chamber members attend these get-togethers with plenty of business cards in tow ready to exchange them with each other. If all goes according to plan, when members eventually need a particular product or service, they simply check their business card file and voilà! They will know whom to go to.

What this intends to accomplish is that Chamber members end up doing business with other Chamber members, in other words, creating a self-sufficient business environment within the membership. It's a great concept and a tremendous ideal. There's only one minor problem: it typically doesn't work. The reason is simply that no matter how loyal a person may be to the Chamber of Commerce, people don't do business with and refer business to business cards. They will most likely only do business with someone for the reason mentioned earlier: All things being equal, people will do business with, and refer business to, those people they know, like, and trust.

Pressing the flesh and handing out an endless number of business cards will not convince people to feel any of these things about you. And most people simply don't know how to cultivate a Chamber audience in such a way as to elicit those feelings. Consider this: Every time you don't create a positive relationship with your one new person, you also don't get the potential business of their 250-person sphere of influence.

Let us now look at the proven techniques that will allow you to take advantage of a wonderful situation, having tons of good prospects right in front of you for about two straight hours. Although we'll use a Chamber of Commerce–type scenario for this example, please realize—and this is very important—these techniques apply to practically all settings, situations, group sizes, and so on.

Expanding Your Client Base the Easy Way

When walking into a typical function (let's make believe this one is an after-hours event, usually running from 5 to 7 P.M.), you basically see the same picture every time. The majority of attendees sit at the bar or hang around the hors d'oeuvres table. They have a few drinks, something to eat, they talk with each other, and they get absolutely nothing done in the way of business. It's basically a party. And maybe even a darn good party at that. But it isn't networking. Many people, however, rationalize that they are indeed networking. They believe they're doing business because they are at this after-normal-business-hours event. About the most productive thing anybody there is doing is every once in a while meeting somebody they don't know and exchanging business cards. Now, no disrespect meant, but . . . big deal!

Occasionally, by sheer luck, some business will take place. One person might just happen to need what another is selling. But the chances of that happening are small, and the odds for success are certainly not being played to their full advantage. Plus, everyone there who is after some business is basically looking at everyone as one new prospect. The difference is that you're now looking at everyone as 250 new prospects. So how do you make these usually social functions become *networking* and work for you? Again, please remember, it is not just these people's businesses you are interested in, but that of their 250-person spheres of influence as well.

The first step is to adjust your attitude—not in the motivational sense of the word, but in the "informational" sense, and that is by realizing that the only reason you are at that particular function is to help your business grow. That doesn't mean it can't be fun. Networking is fun. Establishing mutually beneficial relationships with people is fun. Making more money is fun. But you are there at that card exchange, networking function, cocktail party, social function, or whatever you want to term the occasion, for business purposes.

The second step is to put yourself in the mind-set to appropriately work the crowd. To do this, you have to be the "sincere politician." Be sincere with an air of confidence about you. Be open, but don't come off like a sharp hustler. Be nice, have a smile on your face. Very simple, right? Okay. That's a start.

The third step is to introduce yourself to someone new. A very important point is to introduce yourself to someone who is a center-of-influence-type person. These are the people who have a very large and prestigious sphere of influence. Typically, the center-of-influence types have been in the community for a long time. People are familiar with them, know them, like them, and trust them. These centers of influence themselves may or may not be successful in business. But the point is, they know a lot of other people whom you want to know. Author Rick Hill is an authority on prospecting, and he has a great rule of thumb for locating the function's centers of influence. He notes that people are usually broken up into groups of four, five, or six. According to Hill, each group usually has a dominant person, that one person who seems to control the conversation. He's right. Next time, notice how easy it is to find that one person in every group. When someone in the group makes a point, all heads turn to that person for his or her response. When the dominant person speaks, everyone hangs onto his or her every word. The group laughs when that person laughs. They usually agree with whatever this dominant person says. Remember, that person, although not necessarily financially successful, probably knows a lot of people. Make a point of meeting that person one-on-one. How do you do that, though, if this person is always around other people who are hanging onto his or her every word? Basically, keep your eyes on the few centers of influence as you're walking the perimeter of the room. Eventually, one of them is going to leave his or her present group, maybe to go to the rest room, to get a cocktail, to go to the hors d'oeuvres table, or to possibly even meet some new people. Wait for your opportunity and then walk up and introduce yourself to that person. This is perfectly acceptable behavior for two reasons: that's what everyone is presumably there for, and it isn't as though you're pouncing on that person with a business card. You're simply walking over nicely and introducing yourself.

If you're embarrassed about introducing yourself cold to somebody, it is understandable. Everyone has those feelings at times. But realize that if you simply approach this person politely and not aggressively, this person will usually be quite receptive. Keep in mind, this person knows that everybody, including himself or herself, is there for the purpose of networking. The center of influence is just as anxious to make another contact in you as you are in that person. After exchanging names, ask the center of influence what line of business he or she is in. The center will tell you and ask you the same. Respond briefly with your benefit statement, which is a very short sentence conveying the benefits of what you do, then quickly move on. This will be discussed in detail later.

The fourth step is very, very important. After the introduction, invest 99.9 percent of your conversation asking questions about the center of influence's business. Do not talk about yourself or your business. Why? Because at this point, the center of influence doesn't care about you or your business. Face the facts: your business is probably one of the last things in the world that he or she cares about. That's just the way it is. Centers of influence want to talk about themselves and their business. Let them! This is known as being "you-oriented." Most people, of course, are "me-oriented." Will this get you off to a good start with your networking prospect? Have you ever been in a conversation with someone who let you do practically all the talking? If so, did you say to yourself afterwards, "Wow! What a fascinating conversationalist this person is"? Most people have done that. In fact, isn't it true that the people you find most interesting are the people who seem most interested in you? You bet!

What you need to do is make an impression on the first meeting with a center that will simply elicit the know you, like you, and trust you feelings that are necessary for a mutually beneficial, win-win relationship. You do this by asking questions. The right questions. Incidentally, there's a sneaky kind of danger at this particular point and you need to be aware of it. Let's pretend the person just asked what you do for a living. When you answer, it just happens to be what that person really needs. For instance, you respond with a benefit statement such as "I help people create long-term wealth while providing immediate financial security for their loved ones." Now the person looks at you and miraculously says, "What a coincidence. My spouse and I were just talking about the fact that we are very weak in that area and need to do something about it. After all, we're working hard, but we have no financial future, nothing put away for the later years. We know we definitely need to talk to a person such as yourself right away."

Let's face it. We're only human. At this point, everything inside you wants to go "Yessss!!!!!" That, unfortunately, wouldn't be the correct response. As tempting as it might be to try to set up an appointment with that person and his or her spouse right on the spot, realize that the person is just not ready. The know you, like you, trust you stage has not yet been established.

Bombarding that person right away will do just the opposite of what you want to accomplish. Instead, just go right back to asking questions about the person and his or her business. The type of questions you need to ask are open-ended, feel-good questions. You are probably very familiar with open-ended questions; these are simply questions that cannot be answered with a yes or a no, but require a longer response. Says one sales professional who started his career in television:

I first learned about the importance of open-ended questions when I was a television news anchor for an ABC affiliate in Oklahoma. Management decided that we should have more live interviews during our newscasts, lasting about three minutes. I'm sure when I say "three minutes," that doesn't seem like a particularly long time. On live TV, however, three minutes can be an eternity. Especially when it came to some of the people I interviewed, who, although they may have been very intelligent people, were not used to the bright lights of television and would often find themselves at a loss for words.

For instance, during the oil crisis of the early 1980, I interviewed the president of a local bank. Our conversation ran something like this:

Q: So, Mr. Johnson, how do you feel the current oil situation will affect the local banks as well as the local residents?
A: Uh . . . it's gonna be tough.

Q: Okay . . . it's gonna be tough . . . can you elaborate on that sir?

A: It's going to be real tough.

Now, I would be thinking to myself, "This would be a fantastic time to take a commercial break!" But then I'd hear the director through the earphones screaming, "Stretch, stretch . . . you still have 2 minutes 45 seconds left!" That was tough! But it taught me that if I was going to survive these three-minute live interviews, I needed to learn how to ask questions that would get and keep my guests talking.

What this sales professional did was make a decision to learn from the experts. One valuable idea is to watch some of the top network television interviewers, people such as Ted Koppel, Larry King, and Barbara Walters. These are people who, whether you personally like them or not, know how to ask questions that get people talking.

Barbara Walters, of course, is a bit different. She asks questions that get people crying. That's good! You want to accomplish just the opposite. That's where feel-good questions come into play. You want to ask questions that make people feel good about being in a conversation with you. You want to ask questions that make your new networking prospects feel good about you as a person, even though you've just met and they hardly know you.

Following are ten open-ended, feel-good questions that you can keep in your personal networking arsenal. They are not designed to be probing or salesy in any way. You'll notice that they are all friendly, fun to answer, and will tell you something about the way a person thinks. Mainly, they are questions that will make your new prospect feel good to have the opportunity to answer. Rest assured you'll never need, or have the time, to ask all ten of these questions during any one conversation. Still, you should internalize them. Know them well enough that you are able to ask the ones you deem appropriate for the particular conversation and time frame, without having to actively think about them while your prospect is talking. If you concentrate too much on what you want to say, the person will sense you are not really giving him or her your full attention.

1. *How did you get your start in the business you are in?* Everyone likes to tell their story, don't they? They'd like to be the "Movie of the Week" in someone else's mind. Let them share their story with you while you actively listen.

2. *What do you enjoy most about your profession?* Again, it's a question that elicits a good, positive feeling. And it will get you the positive response you're seeking. This, of course, is much better than the negative alternative: "So tell me, what do you hate most about your job . . . and while we're at it, how about this wretched excuse for a life you live?"

3. *What separates you and your company from the competition?* You can call this the "permission to brag" question. All our lives we're taught not to brag about ourselves and our accomplishments, yet you've just given that person carte blanche to let it all hang out.

4. *What advice would you give someone just starting in your business?* This is what is called your "mentor" question. Doesn't everybody like to feel like a mentor, to feel as though their answer matters? Give that person the chance to feel like a mentor by asking that question.

5. *What one thing would you do with your business if you knew you could not fail?* This question is paraphrased from Dr. Robert Schuller, who asks, "What one thing would you do with your life if you knew you could not fail?" Everybody has a dream, don't they? What is this person's dream? People will appreciate the fact that you

cared enough to ask. They'll always take a few moments to really ponder before they answer.

6. *What significant changes have you seen take place in your profession through the years?* Asking this of people who are a bit more mature in years can be perfect because they love answering it. They've gone through the computer age, the takeover of fax machines, the transition from when service really seemed to matter, and much more.

7. *What do you see as the coming trends in your business?* You can call this the "speculator" question. Aren't people who are asked to speculate usually important, hotshot types on television? You are therefore giving them a chance to be the celebrity, the speculator, and to share their knowledge with you. You're making them feel good about themselves.

8. *Describe the strangest or funniest incident you've experienced in your business.* Give people the opportunity to share their war stories. That's something practically everyone likes to do, isn't it? Don't you have stories you like to share from when you began in business? Something very embarrassing happened that certainly wasn't funny then, but is now. The problem is, most people don't give the person the chance to share it. You, however, are actually volunteering to be that person's audience. Powerful.

9. *What ways have you found to be the most effective for promoting your business?* Again, you are accentuating the positive in this person's mind.

10. *What one sentence would you like people to use in describing the way you do business?* Almost always, people will stop and think really hard before answering that question. What a compliment you've paid them. You've

asked a question that possibly their own loved ones have never thought to ask.

You may be wondering if a person will feel as though you are being nosy asking these questions during a first meeting. The answer is no. First of all, you won't get to ask more than just a few of these questions during your initial conversation anyway. But more important, these are questions people enjoy answering. Remember, the way you ask the questions is critical; you don't want to come off like Mike Wallace of *60 Minutes* conducting an interrogation. These questions are simply meant to be feel-good in nature and establish an initial rapport.

This next question, though, is the most important. This question will separate you from the rest. It is a key step in the process of getting people to feel as though they know you, like you, and trust you. It must be asked smoothly and sincerely, and only after the initial rapport has already been established. The question is, *How can I know if somebody I'm talking to would be a good prospect for you?*

Why is that question so powerful? First of all, just by asking that question, you have separated yourself from the rest of the pack. It is the first indication to that person that you are someone special. You are probably the only person he or she has ever met who asked that question during a first conversation. Or maybe any conversation. Ever. (Most people, of course, simply want to know "What can you do for me?" Oh, they don't come right out and ask that, but isn't that really what they're doing when they start right in with probing questions and hand the person ten business cards, one for them and the others for his or her nine closest friends?)

Have you ever been asked that question or even one similar by somebody you have just met? Perhaps not; very few people can say yes. You have also just informed that person that you are concerned with his or her welfare and wish to contribute to his or her success. Most people would already be trying to sell their own product or service, but not you. You are wondering out loud how you can help. You can be sure that person will have an answer!

Let's say you're talking to Gary, who sells copying machines to businesses. He's very successful and an obvious center of influence. You ask, "Gary, *how can I know if somebody I'm talking to would be a good prospect for you?*" He'll probably respond with something similar to "If you ever happen to be in an office, you might notice the copying machine. If you see that the wastepaper basket next to it is filled to the rim, and even overflowing with crumpled up pieces of paper, that's a sure sign that copying machine has not been working well lately, and that could be an excellent prospect for me."

Don't we all have ways to know when someone may be a good prospect whom the general public does not know? People you meet from now on will be glad to share their knowledge in that area with you. And don't you think they'll appreciate your sincere interest? You bet they will! Eventually, you'll put that information to use for your center's benefit, and especially for yours. One thing you know to be true is this: the best way to get business and get referrals is to give business and give referrals. This is only the beginning of the networking process. Again, that one key question will be the first real indication to the person that you are somebody special and different, a person worthy of doing business with, directly, or by way of referrals. Learn that question word-for-word until it becomes part of you, and you could ask it, as the saying goes, "in your sleep."

You will find that by asking you-oriented questions, you will establish excellent contacts on planes en route from one city to another. Says one MDRT sales professional:

> On one occasion, I kept a person talking about himself for the last hour and forty-five minutes of the flight. Yes, that took some concentration on my part. As we landed I said, "If I can

ever refer business your way, I definitely will." He replied, "Me too," and I could tell he meant it. Then, with an embarrassed smile, he asked, "By the way, what do you do?" Amazing. Just by my focusing on him, he was totally sold on me without even knowing anything about me.

Another time, I was sitting next to a syndicated columnist on a flight from Chicago to San Francisco. I asked all about her and her career as a journalist. The result? A feature story on me and my business that ran in all the papers that syndicate her column. This works!

So, your conversations with your new networking prospects have concluded, and you hardly mentioned yourself and what you do for a living. That's okay, as long as you have their business cards. Be sure that before you part company, you ask for their cards. They'll give them to you. Remember, they are looking at you as a prospect. If they ask for your card, give it to them, but realize that your card probably will be thrown out at that person's earliest convenience. Let's put it this way: your card will either be thrown out directly, or it will travel through a never-ending dimension of time and space forever lost in the "Rolodex zone."

The sixth step will actually happen a bit later in the event you are attending. By this time, you may already have met several people and have gone through steps one through five with each of them. Now, when you run into one of them at the food table, be sure and acknowledge the center by name. Let's say it's half an hour or forty-five minutes later, and you're standing at the hors d'oeuvres table. You very pleasantly say, "Hi (Center's first name)," or better yet, "Hi, Mr./Ms (Center's last name), are you having a nice time, enjoying yourself?" That's really going to be impressive, especially because he or she, by this time, has more than likely forgotten your name. It's almost a guarantee that at that point, he or she will take notice of your name. Remembering people's names and faces is a very valuable skill, and one that virtually anyone can learn. There are several good books on the subject. The time you invest in learning that skill will pay big dividends.

The seventh step is to introduce people you have met to others, preferably, people who can be of mutual benefit to one another. You should be able to make several good contacts at these meetings. So introduce these people to each other. This is called "creative matchmaking." Position yourself as a center of influence, the one who knows the movers and shakers. People will respond to that, and you'll soon become what you project. Give each person a nice introduction and explanation as to what the other does. Suggest ways they can look for leads for each other. Remember what was discussed in the fourth step: ask people how you can know if a person you're talking to can be a good prospect for them. Tell the center what would be a good lead for another person, and vice versa. Wow! Will he or she be impressed! The center is going to be reminded that you cared enough about him or her to really listen and remember. It will show sincere interest on your part and that will make those people more interested in helping you. All this time, you're just beginning to give them a hint of the fact that you are an ace, one with whom to do or refer business.

A nice touch is to politely excuse yourself partway through the conversation, and leave the two of them talking to each other. Guess what and who they'll start talking about? You, and how impressed they are with you. Of course, another way you can ensure meeting people with whom you can have mutually beneficial networking relationships is to introduce yourself to people involved in your target markets. For instance, if you're looking to create a niche in the real estate market, obviously you want to meet and network with realtors, especially with the realtors who have strong centers of influence. How will you know that a person is a realtor before introducing yourself? Be creative. You can check a directory or guest list beforehand if one is available and

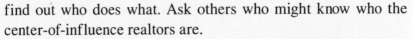
find out who does what. Ask others who might know who the center-of-influence realtors are.

Another method is name tags. You may have spotted a real estate company name on a name tag as you passed by someone. Or you might have accidentally overheard a part of his or her conversation with someone else, indicating that person is a realtor. You'll find a way to know.

Now the business function has ended. Hopefully, you've met about five or six good contacts. Even one or two would not be bad. That's all you need. One or two good ones are much better than just handing out a bunch of business cards to people with whom you will never end up doing business. That's what everyone else was doing. You've taken a different, more personal approach. The scenario is now set for the follow-up.

Follow-Up Techniques

Thus far, you've done well in finding and meeting your networking prospects, in this example, through a business-after-hours meeting, but it could have been practically anywhere else. The point is, you've made a great, positive impression on those you've met. Now comes the follow-up. By systematically and consistently implementing the following techniques, you will separate yourself, a successful networker, from everyone else. You're probably thinking that follow-up is a royal pain. It can be, but only if you do a lot of unnecessary, time-consuming tasks that don't get results.

Once you internalize these techniques as good habits, they will not seem like hardships. But they will help you build or add to your already powerful network. This will result in a lot of referral business.

The first step in the follow-up process is to send a personalized Thank-you note. Sure you've been taught that in Basic Sales Training 101; however, very few people actually do this, not realizing they are missing out on an important step. Or, they'll try it a few times, and if they don't get immediate gratification, they'll stop doing it and say it doesn't work. But it does work, if done correctly. People who send the type of notes that are about to be described, which are different and much more profitable than the usual ones, get remembered for several reasons: Primarily, you'll stand out from the competition, because you are one of the few doing this. And the recipient will actually see who it is sending that note. More on that in a moment.

Regarding the type of stationery and design for the note card you send, use an individually designed postcard that measures 8½ by 3½ inches. In the top right-hand corner should be your company name and logo. Beneath the logo is your photo. Just beneath the photo is your name. Below that, your company address and telephone number. All of this is on the right-hand side of the postcard, leaving plenty of room for writing the note. Across the bottom is your short benefit statement, such as "Create long-term wealth while providing immediate security for your loved ones." This note should be a nonpushy, simple, brief note, written in blue ink (research indicates that blue ink is more effective both in business and personally) that says something to the effect of, "Hi (Center's name), thank you. It was a pleasure meeting you. If I can ever refer business your way, I certainly will." Let's look at what you've done. You have shown:

- ✓ Professionalism.
- ✓ A lot of class.
- ✓ That you are conscientious.
- ✓ That you are a person worthy of doing business with directly or having business referred to.

What you didn't do was come on strong and try to hard sell. You simply thanked the person just for the meeting (you like to be thanked, don't you?). You also let that person know once again that you have his or her best interests in mind, with the promise to make an effort to send business that person's way. It is strongly suggested that you make no mention of what you do or your desire to provide the person or anyone he or she knows with your services. First of all, that would be contrary to all you've done thus far. Second, the person will know what you do for a living from the benefit statement at the bottom of the card. He or she understands why you sent the note and is already impressed with you.

Sometimes, the more you understate your case, the more dramatic an impact you make. Besides, you're going to give people plenty of opportunities to be thinking of you in the very near future. That photo, by the way, is very important: you want them to know who sent the note, and without your photo, they might not remember meeting you. People often meet many other people during the course of a day. As impressed as they were with you during the meeting, they will easily forget you after you have left. As the saying goes, "out of sight, out of mind." What you're doing is giving them a quick reminder right off the bat.

As human beings, we think in pictures. Now, if you have ever studied neurolinguistic programming, or NLP, then you know that we process information in three different ways: auditorily, which is by sound; visually, by sight; and kinesthetically, which is by touch or feeling. Nonetheless, humans *think* in pictures.

If you don't believe that, then right now, do not, absolutely do not think of a purple elephant. What comes to your mind right now? Most likely, a purple elephant! Bet you are fighting it awfully hard right now, aren't you?

The fact is, human beings think in pictures, so use that to your advantage. Although this is only the first step toward having prospects see your face whenever they or someone they know needs your products and services, it is still an important step. For maximum effectiveness, put your photo on this postcard. Any black-and-white photo will do just fine. Ask your local printer to typeset and have this postcard professionally printed. The expense is minimal, and the payback is well worth it.

Now, back to the sending of this note. It's suggested that you enclose it in a regular #10 envelope. Hand-address the envelope (again, in blue ink), as opposed to typing it. Do not put a mailing label on it, or on anything else you want the person receiving the information to open. Many people, while opening their daily mail, quickly look at envelopes and sort out what looks like junk mail so they can quickly throw out those pieces. You don't want your letter mistaken for that, do you? Hand-stamp the envelope, as opposed to using a postage meter. An even nicer touch is to use a large, oversized commemorative stamp. In other words, personalize it. Make it special so that the receiver wants to open the envelope quickly. You want this envelope to be opened and the message actually read. If it looks like junk mail, it could be thrown out before ever having been opened. A hand-addressed, hand-stamped envelope will grab people's attention more effectively than one with an impersonal mailing label and postage meter.

Because you've done it the right way, let's examine the recipient's probable response. He or she sees the envelope the next morning. Because it appears to be a personal letter, the person will open it. Chances are, he or she still won't, at this point, even associate you with the company name on the envelope. Remember, "out of sight . . ."

Now, as your networking prospect pulls out your postcard note and sees your picture, he or she remembers the good feelings associated with you. You are the one who focused on him or her. You made this person feel important. You asked how you could help this person find new business, and even introduced him or her to others. Mainly, you made that person feel good about himself or herself.

However, now the recipient thinks: Here comes the solicitation. "If I can ever sell you, or someone you know, let me know."

But you didn't do that, correct? Far from it! All you did was say thank you for the meeting and let the person know you'll try to refer business his or her way. The person will certainly appreciate you for thinking that highly of him or her, and will remember the effort.

You might be thinking, But I'm too busy. I don't have time to write a thank-you note to every new, good networking prospect I meet. The answer is, Yes, you do! The pros, the champions, the ones who are successful and looking to be even more successful do the little things right, and do them consistently. That includes writing and sending these postcard notes. Those sales professionals who are committed to realizing the benefits of effective networking write them even when they don't want to.

Here's a shortcut you can use that will make the process even a bit easier: During some down time, simply take twenty-five or thirty of your blank, personalized postcard notes. Leave room at the top for the salutation, and write, "Thank you, it was a pleasure meeting you. If I can ever refer business your way, I certainly will." And sign your name. Put an elastic band around the postcards and place them neatly in a shoe box inside the trunk of your car, along with an equal number of already hand-stamped envelopes. You could also hire your child or an assistant who has good handwriting to do this for you. From now on, whenever you meet new networking prospects, simply go to your car, write their name at the top of the note, hand-write their name and address on the envelope (that's why you took their business card), and drop it in the nearest mailbox. Sure, it's still a little bit of extra work, but as speaker and best-selling author Zig Ziglar says, "You don't pay the price of success, you enjoy the benefits of success."

Keep in mind that sending the note is simply a way of establishing yourself and your credibility with this person. It usually will not get immediate results; however, that's not to say *never*. As one MDRT sales professional remembers, "It reminds me of a time when I was younger. I had accompanied an older friend, an excellent bowler, to the alleys one night for a game of 10-pin bowling. It really struck me how he'd get strike after strike. Wow! I commented on how it must be a lot of fun and how hard he must have worked on nailing those strikes. He replied that the key is not to concentrate on nailing the strikes, but on nailing the spares, the various splits formed from the pins left standing after the first ball. 'Once you learn to master nailing the spares' he advised, 'the strikes will come by themselves.'"

His was an example of great wisdom. Master sending the notes correctly and promptly for future business, and the immediate business will come by itself. So don't forget: a simple note or two can do wonders when it comes to networking. Don't you love getting thank-you notes? You always tend to remember those who send them.

Next, send any articles, newspaper or magazine clippings, or other pieces of information that relate to your networking prospects or their business. If you hear something that may be helpful to them, send it on your personalized postcard note.

For example, a networking prospect sells temporary services to businesses. You hear a rumor that a large company is about to open in a certain building. That would make an excellent informational note that would be very appreciated, wouldn't it? You could simply call the person or drop a note. Sending that note is so effective and memorable and will work to your advantage. You could write "Mary, a quick note to let you know Amalgamated International is about to open in XYZ building. Thought it would be a good prospective lead. Good luck." Then sign your name. Now, can't you see how the person on the receiving end of that note would appreciate your unselfish gesture?

Here's a personal example from some years back from an MDRT professional in a local direct-sales business:

One prospect, in particular, was definitely a center-of-influence person whose referrals I was very much interested in.

He was also a direct prospect, as he owned and ran a local franchise business. One morning in the newspaper, I saw a rather uncomplimentary article about that franchise at its national level. This can be a rather touchy situation because we don't want to send our people bad news. However, I cut the article out of the paper and wrote a note on my postcard saying, "Although I don't agree with the article, I thought it would still be of interest to you." I enclosed the article and note in an envelope and sent it to the direct prospect.

He called the very next day to thank me for my consideration and thoughtfulness. He hadn't seen the article and was glad I cared enough to send it. In fact, he planned to write a rebuttal letter to the editor as a result, which he did. Let me ask you, did I get his business that day? No. But I did two months later, when he was ready.

In other words, when my products or services were needed by that person, I was the only one who would naturally come to his mind. The founder of the National Speakers Association, Cavett Robert, said it best: "People don't care how much you know, until they know how much you care, about them, and their problems."

After knowing how much I cared, he was more than willing to find out how much I knew. Over time, I also received numerous referrals from him. Sending newspaper or magazine articles affecting our networking prospects on a personal level is also a very valuable idea. I know, it's another point we all learned in Basic Sales 101, but how many people actually do it, consistently?

One challenge sales professionals might create for themselves in this area is limiting their horizons. You might be thinking, "Well, how often does someone in my network actually get their name or picture in the newspaper? Maybe the Business Monday section if they got promoted or something, but how often does that happen?"

Here's a suggestion: as you look through the newspaper, scour it to see what bits and pieces of news or information somehow, in some way, affect those in your network. If something you read has anything to do with them, their profession, personal interests, hobbies, whatever, send it, along with a short note.

Maybe Diane is an avid antique collector, and you see an article in your newspaper that a new antique store is about to open in town. Send her a note to let her know. She'll appreciate your thinking of her without first needing her for something.

The next step in the networking process is one of the best ideas we've ever come across; we learned about it seven or eight years ago. Simply, send your networking prospects a note pad, otherwise known as a scratch pad, every few months or so to keep you on their mind. This note pad should contain your company name, logo, and your photo, with your name directly beneath the photo, just as on the postcard. Your address and telephone number should also be included. Be sure to keep all the information about you on the top quarter of the page. That way, recipients have plenty of room to write their notes. Otherwise, of course, they'll throw it out.

Scratch pads, or note pads, are used by virtually everyone, whether in their home or office. When they can constantly see your photo, you become familiar to them. Prospects are going to have your face right in front of them a lot of the time. Your visibility and credibility will increase in their mind. You see, what you really want is for them to be thinking of you and only you whenever anything is ever brought up concerning your business. As a life insurance professional, you want them to think of you whenever "insurance" comes up in a conversation.

Once, my director of marketing called a prospect on the other side of the country, because she knew it was planning time for their annual convention. The moment my name was mentioned, the meeting planner said, "Oh yes, I have his note pad right here on my desk. How's he doing?" Please keep in mind, I had, at that time, never personally spoken to that meeting planner. Neverthe-less, she felt she knew me by virtue of seeing my picture every sin-gle working day.

Oh yes, we got the booking. Don't get me wrong, however; I'm sure the decision to have me present a program at their con-vention was not based solely on the note pad. What I am certain of is that it at least opened up the door, kept me in the ball game, and kept the benefits of my program on that person's mind.

You see, when that pad with your picture is seen by prospects constantly, here's what happens: every time they see your name, they see your face and they know what you do for a living. Every time they see your face, they also know your name and what you do for a living. And most important, every time they or some-body they know needs what you do for a living, they know your name and they know your face.

It also works the opposite way. Ethel is a realtor and a member of a large office. She has lived in her community all of her life, and is very well liked and respected. One day, she ran into a woman with whom she had been friends for years. The woman ex-citedly said, "Ethel, you're going to be real happy to know I've just listed my home for sale with one of the salespeople in your of-fice." Ethel, for reasons easy to understand, was not exactly de-lighted by that news. She nicely, but disappointedly, asked, "But we've known each other for years. Why didn't you list it with me?" The woman, now realizing the situation, replied, "Ethel, I'm so sorry. I just didn't think of you at the time." What that shows is that people generally don't care about our success as much as we care about our success. That isn't surprising. People are concerned with their own lives and their own problems. If we are not some-how in front of them at the very time of a buying decision (whether they are buying directly or in a position to refer busi-ness), there's a chance they may not think of us until it's too late.

We've got to keep ourselves in front of our networking prospects constantly. Of course, we must accomplish this in a very nonpushy, nonthreatening, almost subliminal manner. The goal is to be the only one they think of when it comes time for them or anyone in their sphere of influence to need or want our products and services.

Newsletters, pens, magnets, and other promotional items are fine. They can never hurt. The problem is that either their shelf life isn't long, as in the case of the newsletter, or they don't have your picture on them and can't always be seen by your networking prospect anyway. A pen will run out of ink and be thrown away, and there goes your name and phone number. The scratch pad will be kept and used.

A key step is to refer as much business as you possibly can to those in your established and new network. Have as a goal to position yourself as a referral source throughout your network. It was mentioned earlier that the best way to get business and get referrals is to give business and give referrals.

Once you get into the habit, it's extremely simple and easy. For instance, from now on, every time you ever meet or come across anyone who has a particular need, ask yourself, Who do I know in my network that can fulfill that need? I'm sure that you know who you would refer as an accountant, a dentist, a chiropractor, an electrician, or practically anything else, don't you? Every time you help people get their need fulfilled, they'll appreciate you that much more. And every time you bring people a referral, you know they'll appreciate you even more. After a while, not only does it become habit forming, but people begin to think of you as the person who knows the right people and has the answers. It will position you solidly, and people will want to make you happy knowing you are a great source of potential referrals to them.

The next step is when you receive a referral. Be sure and follow up every time, immediately, with a handwritten, personalized note of thanks. We suggest using the personalized postcards format discussed earlier.

The note should read something along the lines of "Dear Mary, thank you so much for your nice referral of Bob Jones. You can be assured that anyone you refer to me will be treated with the utmost caring and professionalism." Now isn't that effective? Short, sweet, professional, and to the point. It says it all. Not to mention, it will surely reaffirm the referrer's feeling that you were the right person to whom he or she should have given that referral.

Of course, depending on the situation, you can alter the wording of the note or even the type of thank you. Send flowers to people who have given you valuable referrals. It's certainly worth the investment. And it's a nice way of saying thank you to someone you genuinely like, and to whom you feel grateful.

However you thank someone, do it in a way that separates you from the rest. Constantly show that person why you should be the only one in your field receiving the referrals of his or her 250-person sphere of influence.

So far, we have talked about how to go about, in a very non-pushy, nonaggressive, nonthreatening way, getting people to have good feelings about you: getting them to know you, like you, and trust you; wanting to see you succeed and wanting to help you find new business. The challenge is, even though they may have these positive feelings, they might not know how to help you find new business. The type of work you do might seem obvious to you; however, it might not be obvious to them. And even if they understand what you do, knowing how to network for you and help you find new business is a different story.

What you need to do is make it easy for them to know how to refer business to you. Effectively train the people who want to network for you. First off, once you've got somebody ready to be your walking ambassador, make sure he or she knows the benefits of what you do, not just the features. All of us know the difference between a feature and a benefit. A feature is what something is. A benefit is what it does for that person.

For instance, insurance, in and of itself, is a feature; financial wealth and security is the benefit. "I sell life insurance" is a feature. On the other hand, "I help people create wealth while providing immediate security for their loved ones" is a benefit. Maybe you would prefer, "I help people prepare for a sound financial future, while protecting themselves and their loved ones for the present." Either benefit statement might work for you, or maybe neither of them feels quite right. Work on creating one that fits what you are trying to accomplish.

Your benefit statement should take no more than five to seven seconds. Make the benefits recognizable enough so that your networking associate can easily determine the want or need in others. We suggest that you develop this benefit statement and practice it on people you know. Allow them to critique and evaluate the statement.

Often, this benefit statement will start off along the lines of "I show people how to" or "I help people to." Usually, it isn't good to use "I" at the beginning of a sentence, though in this case, you have to, unless you can come up with something different.

What's vital is that you show where you help somebody do something or you do something for somebody. You see, eventually, after you have gained people's confidence, and they want to network for you, you can mention to them that you could use their help. Or they may actually say to you, "What can I do for you now that you've been such a help to me? You've thrown me business, you've thought of me, how can I know if somebody I'm talking to would be a good prospect for you?" And you can train them how to network for you. Another idea is to invite to lunch a center-of-influence person with whom you've established a true networking relationship. Assure the person that you are going to continue to network for him or her. At the same time, over lunch, show and teach that person how to network for you as well.

That brings us to another point: how to ask for referrals in such a way that you actually get them. Have you ever said to somebody immediately after helping him or her, or even at the point where you really felt good about this person wanting to help you, "Do you know anybody else who could benefit from my services?" And the person thought about it, and thought in earnest, and finally said, "Well, I can't think of anybody right now, but when I do, I'll definitely let you know." And then you never heard from him or her again regarding a referral.

It wasn't that person's fault. He or she was given too large a frame of reference with which to work. Instead, as Tom Hopkins teaches, what you need to do is isolate or funnel down the world into just a few people that your prospects can see. Remember, as human beings we think in pictures.

Think of isolating this way: Has anybody ever asked you if you knew a good joke? Now, you probably have heard and know plenty of good jokes, but can you ever actually think of one when someone asks you?

One night, I called my local oldies radio station; that's my kind of music. I called to request the song "Only in America" by Jay and the Americans. The announcer told me they no longer carry that song on their play list. "But," he asked, "do you happen to know any other oldies you would like to hear?" Now, I know hundreds of oldies I'd like to hear, but could I think of even one at that moment? No way!

It's virtually the same situation when we ask people if they know anybody who could benefit from our products or services. They most likely know plenty of people who could, or who might, but try to get them to think of even one person at that time using that approach and it's probably not going to happen. Instead, give them a frame of reference. For instance, "Gary, you were telling me you're an avid golfer. Is there a specific foursome you play with most of the time?" "Well, yeah, there's Joe Martin, Ken Stevens, and Nancy Goldblatt." "Great. Would any of them happen to"—and then you get into the benefits of what you do.

Maybe none of them would be good referrals, so you head into another direction and a different scenario. Gary is also a member of Rotary. Keep in mind that we don't just want to ask "Do you know anybody in the organization who might," because "anybody" is too large a frame of reference. We need to narrow the focus. Instead, we might ask, "Gary, who in your Rotary Club do you sit with most of the time?" "Dave Johnson and Karen Henderson are probably my two closest friends in Rotary," he replies. So you ask, "Would either of them be . . . ?"

Let's move on to one more frame of reference with Gary. You know he sits on the board of directors of his local office products association. You might ask, "Gary, how many people serve on your board with you?" "Five." Five is okay in this instance because he knows them and can picture them. Maybe one of them might be a good prospect for you.

But here's the key: by giving him people he can see, the pressure is off of him to have to think of people out of thin air. Pressure hurts the memory. Even if none of the people he has named are good prospects, the chances are that someone will come to mind. And once he comes up with one name, he'll naturally begin thinking of others.

So, in effect, you're limiting the number of potential people your prospects might know but are increasing the number of referrals you'll actually receive. Very effective.

Although we've just scratched the surface of networking techniques, I truly hope you feel you've gotten some useful information that you can take with you and begin applying immediately. I wish each of you the best of continued success . . . AND GREAT NETWORKING!

The Million Dollar Business Card

The following is some sound advice from a top MDRT sales associate regarding business cards and their impact on prospecting:

I want to tell you some of the things I do to meet new prospects, with my business card being the prime factor. If you were to look at my business card, you would notice it's small in size. My name is presented on the front, and on the back it reads, "The size of this card is made necessary by the amount of business you've given me lately."

I also have a regulation business card, like most sales professionals. It reads, "Life insurance, employee benefits, health insurance, etc." Usually, when I give it out to prospects, it is thrown away within a matter of seconds after I leave the room. So I decided to make a different kind of a business card. It reads on the front, "When you're looking for the best, give me a ring." And the card chimes when you open it. Isn't that fabulous? Those regulation cards can be purchased for a penny each and get little or no results. Yet, when you spend $4 for a card that chimes, no one ever throws it away. What do they do? They show it to twenty-five or thirty people: "Listen to this card this guy gave me. It rings in your ear, listen. It rings." And they don't throw it away. So it makes a lot of sense.

I also have another card called "My Yellow Pages." These are the numbers you can reach me at because I believe in the philosophy that you promise a lot and deliver even more. So, I give prospects and clients all my phone numbers: my corporate office number, my private office number, my toll-free number, my voice mailbox number, my car phones, my fax machine, and my home phone. And I say to them, "If you can't get me at one of these numbers, call Goldstein's Funeral Home. I'm in one of those wooden boxes."

Take a look at my briefcase; you might find something unusual. I carry lots of pens, highlighters, and pencils with my name imprint. It's a prospecting technique. When you see new prospects, they usually ask you why you have so many pens in your bag. I take one out and say, "It reminds me to ask for referrals. Would you take a pen and please write down the name of somebody like you whom I can talk to." The pen is not for them, it's for me.

Referrals: A Gold Mine of Opportunity

For many sales professionals, referrals are the number-one factor in their business success. Why develop such an indirect prospecting system? Why not just contact prospects directly? Why get third-party sources involved, especially those that can control access to potential clients? Why decide that "power lead referrals," often referred to as "center-of-influence marketing," are the ideal source of new clients?

Is it because your case count will increase? Or because you can write them more quickly and hopefully turn the classic formula of ten prospects to three hot leads to one sale into the dream formula of 1-1-1? All of these reasons may be valid, but the real reason is that many sales professionals suffer from rejection reluctance!

Rejection reluctance is related to call reluctance and, although not immediately fatal, it can (if not properly dealt with) have a limiting effect on your career. You must understand that when people say no, they aren't rejecting you personally. For many sales associates, rejection feels just the same as when they were younger, only now they know why the word no hurts, and they try not to take it personally.

Knowing why something hurts doesn't make the pain any less, but it can make it tolerable if the long-term goal is important enough. One of the differences between human beings and other animals is our ability to make purposeful, long-term changes. Humans can choose to endure short-term pain for longer-term rewards. But, if you could reach your goal with no pain at all, that would be an even better strategy.

You, like many sales associates, may have more skills, education, and training than your production shows. You may feel good when you open a sale, fact-find a need, design a solution, or close a sale. Almost all sales associates feel good when they are more effective. Yet, when you analyze it, the part of the business you most likely dislike is the rejection you encounter when prospecting for new business.

A solution for combating rejection is the development of a marketing program that positions your product or services through centers of influence. This system will allow you to accomplish your goals while minimizing the pain of rejection.

A marketing system based on referrals can work for you because it is transferable, and because it is based on a fundamental law of human nature: people want to help those they like and care for. Think about the last referral you gave someone; didn't you do it because you knew that by introducing these two people to each other it would produce a win-win situation for both of them?

That was the conclusion of one MDRT sales associate when he referred a fee-only financial planner to a client of his several years back. "Over a period of time," he said, "I had gotten to know the planner, and I had developed confidence in her abilities, methods, and motives. I knew that she had the skill to make my client happy. Putting these two together would benefit both of them and me in the long run."

Looking at it from centers' point of view, they have clients who need your products and services. But for them to feel comfortable referring to you, you must become a trusted resource to the centers, one who has both the skills and the integrity to help their friends and associates when it comes to the product or service you sell. Once trust and confidence are established, the referrals will follow.

You might ask yourself, Can I do this as a sole practitioner, or do I have to be part of a larger organization? The type of organization is not the key! The key is persistence and the faith necessary to implement a program that can take several years. People refer to people, not to companies or organizations. Referrals are a function of relationships and trust between people. People will trust your organization (if you have one) only after they've formed a personal relationship with you.

Disadvantages of Using Centers of Influence

There are three main disadvantages to adopting a centers-of-influence-approach system:

1. *It takes a long time before you get any payback.* It can take as long as five years before you get your first good referral. Most good sales associates don't have that kind of patience. Our culture, training, and natural inclination is to want immediate results. The centers-of-influence system is a long-term process that will work only over an extended period of time.

   Trust is the key element. CPAs, attorneys, and others, for that matter, will not refer anyone to you unless they trust you, your knowledge, and your motives completely. One sales associate explained how he learned about the power of transferred trust during a closing interview with a couple who had been referred to him by their attorney. During the closing interview, when it was time to sign the applications, the sales associate instinctively handed the forms to the attorney so he could give them to his clients for their signatures. It was only later that the significance of this action dawned on him. The clients had a long-term and trusting relationship with their attorney and, as a consequence, they trusted anyone their attorney trusted, in this case, the sales associate they had never met and didn't know.

   In our culture, perception becomes a reality. That is why, in public surveys, people don't perceive of salespeople in the best light. However, when asked if they have had a close, trusting relationship with any particular salesperson, those who say yes say their sales professional is different: he or she listens, explains things, and tries to meet their needs. What's the difference? A relationship has been formed over time, and customers have learned to trust the salesperson and his or her motives.

2. *Loss of control.* Most successful sales professionals are selected and trained not only because they have a high sense of urgency, but because they are doers, catalysts. They make things happen, and they like to take charge. Unfortunately, many centers of influence demand a long-term attitude and dogged persistence if a strategy is to work. Sales associates must allow control to remain with the center of influence. They have to take on supportive roles to help centers solve their clients' problems. This secondary role may be new to you and require a change in attitude. As a sales associate, you must be careful not to take over.

3. *To be successful using a centers-of-influence approach, you must be willing to change roles.* Your new role becomes one of support, to educate the center and his or her friends or associates so that they can make informed decisions based on knowledge. You must become part of the center of influence's research team: accessible, accurate, and dependable. You must develop trust so that you can receive what is often referred as the "power referral."

There is a hierarchy of referrals, from a mere name, where the referrer has no status or stature with the referee; to a high-quality referral, where the referrer is well thought of and respected by referee; to a "power referral," where the referrer is in a position of trust, influence, and possibly control over the referee. Your job becomes easy if people will let you get close enough to help them. It is developing this trust that takes time, effort, and commitment to a long-term relationship. It is also why it takes so much time to turn a prospect into a buyer of your products or services. The big sales come later, when the client knows you have his or her best interest at heart. The prospects have all the necessary prerequisites:

need, desire, money, and trust. It should not take extraordinary skills or abilities to help this kind of prospect.

These are the results this system will produce in time, and there are two additional benefits:

1. Some centers will become clients.

2. You will become recognized as an expert in your community.

A number of these CPAs, attorneys, bankers, stockbrokers, and others will themselves become clients. You may find that when explaining your background and areas of expertise and those of your firm during a low-key, information-only interview, centers will often ask for information and help on their own product needs. In addition, some of your best centers may start out as personal clients.

By using the techniques about to be described, you will become known as an expert in your community, and this has a number of benefits:

1. When you are a well-regarded expert, there is no need to bring in another sales professional for a second opinion.

2. Other sales professionals, hearing you are involved with a prospect or client, won't bother to compete.

3. There will be numerous opportunities for joint work with less experienced sales professionals.

The "How to's" of Developing Centers of Influence for Referrals

Let's begin by defining your "target" prospects and the goals for a referral program. Your goal should be to develop a group of people who can and will consistently refer quality prospects who have a need for the product or service you are selling. These prospects should have a good relationship with the center and see him or her as a person of value, whose advice they actively seek and follow. Therefore, when you are referred, you also should be seen as a person of potential value to the prospect. The strength of the referral should make prospects open up to you during the fact-finding, so that they share their real concerns and objectives. With complete facts, designing a solution to their needs is usually not that difficult.

Marketing to centers of influence can be broken down into two basic technique types: defensive and offensive. Defensive marketing takes more money than time. It is designed to create an image or impression in the mind of the client or center of influence, one of expertise and experience. Defensive techniques are designed to go out to both a large and broad audience.

For one MDRT sales professional, the idea of defensive marketing was introduced early in his career: "I had a practice of asking top sales associates if I could spend a day with them," he says. "My goal was to learn from them so I could incorporate what I could into my own practice. Over the years, I was able to spend time with superstar-caliber sales associates. It was during a trip to Vancouver, B.C., that I noticed one of these superstars had built the reputation of his firm into that of the most knowledgeable in the city. He did this by simply performing an in-house seminar once a year for each of the then top-eight CPA firms. This was my first exposure to image building and market positioning, and I determined to create my own program."

Following are ten specific examples he implemented in his program—and continues to use to reach both centers of influence and prospects.

Advertising

He decided to start his image-building program by placing regular ads in professional journals and magazines. This type of advertising was designed to position his company in the center's mind as an old and well-established firm. "People seem to think that if you have the money to pay for institutional ads, you must have been around a long time," he states. These ads were designed to build name recognition; they were not designed to sell directly but rather "to link us and our firm to the products and services we offer." When people mention having seen his ads, they always ask him to tell them what it is he does; then he knows the ads are effective. "For my business, CPAs and attorneys are my best centers, so I run ads in statewide publications referring to either," he says. "In addition, I advertise in a local athletic club that has fourteen resident members. These ads run a minimum of six to twelve times a year in each magazine. The text of the ad, the layout, and the photos are changed on a regular basis to keep client attention.

Mailers

He also uses two different mailers to keep his name, face, firm's name and logo, as well as what he does in front of the center on a monthly basis. "My criteria for the mailer is that it be prepared by a third party and have good content and room for my photo, name, corporate logo, my company's mission statement, and a theme line, 'Innovative Ideas for Profitable Companies and Professionals since 1975.'"

In addition, he stays in contact with his centers by mailing a personal note with photocopies of relevant newspaper articles, magazine articles, and anything he feels his centers might find of interest.

Broadcast Fax

This idea was derived from a member of his study group. This associate was pulling articles off the Internet and broadcast-faxing them to clients and centers of influence. "A number of us liked the idea but had concerns about copyright violations," he says. "Another member of the study group decided we could avoid the problem by summarizing the articles. A number of us financed the start-up costs. So each month, I get a computer disc with two of the bimonthly 'Just the Fax' one-pagers using my name, logo, and phone number on the header."

Both mailers and broadcast faxes are designed to go to a very large number of people. He says he has well over a thousand people on his two lists.

Third-Party Public Relations

Public relations is a method of shaping public opinion. One of the best ways to enhance your image and reputation is to be quoted, as an expert, in the business section of your local newspaper, business journal, or industry magazine. By cultivating editors and reporters, the associate gets quoted favorably in most articles related to the products he sells.

He works at cultivating these editors and reporters the same way he does other centers of influence. "I meet with them two or three times a year for breakfast or lunch, and put them on my mailing and broadcast fax lists," he says. "I also invite them to be my guest at topical seminars or meetings of interest to them. Over time, they begin to view me as a resource for articles that involve the products and services I am associated with, and I get quoted in their periodicals."

Write Articles for Their Journals

This MDRT sales professional also contacts the editors of his state Bar Association magazine and takes them to lunch. "I give them my background and volunteer to write an article on a subject of interest to their members." If you need help, you can ask your company's marketing department (if applicable) to help you. If all else fails, do the research yourself. But remember: if your article comes from one source, that's plagiarizing, but if it comes from many sources, that's research.

Speak at Their Meetings

Over a two-year period, this MDRT member has spoken at two annual meetings of the state CPA society and the local Bar Association. His speeches have covered a wide variety of subjects. In each instance, he either was invited to speak by a member of the program committee who knew him or he was recommended by someone who knew him.

"What I didn't know at the time," he says, "was the effect this had on my image among my peers. I had simply viewed it as a way to give back to the industry, but it also made other sales professionals who were competitors bow out when they heard I was working with a prospect, because of my perceived knowledge and experience."

Exhibit at Annual Meetings

Find out if your industry's state-level or annual conventions have exhibitors. If so, attend as an exhibitor. If you have never done this before, consider hiring a meeting or exhibit consultant. This is a very unique form of promotion and requires the help of an expert to get the most from the meeting. "I began with a consultant, who helped me design my exhibit, trained my staff, and helped us avoid learning everything the hard way," he recalls. If you are interested in doing this, spend some time talking to veteran exhibitors at a local conference.

Briefings

The original concept of briefing is one that the sales associate heard from a peer at an industry forum. It is designed to increase the number of centers who can refer business to your firm. "Originally, it worked like this," he says:

My partner or I would invite a CPA or attorney to join us for breakfast or lunch. We would ask him or her to bring other partners that worked in the same or complementary areas that we hadn't met yet. The first meeting was always breakfast or lunch and was frequently held in a private dining room of our Athletic Club.

Because we work in three distinct product areas, we asked other staff members from those areas to attend as well. We introduced ourselves, went over our firm's brochure, and asked them how we could be of help either to them or their clients. My goal was not only to add new centers to our mailing and broadcast fax list, but to get the firm to agree to allow us to put on two to four one-hour seminars in their conference room each year. These in-house briefings cover the basics of the more advanced uses of the products and services we sell. The goal is to demonstrate knowledge and willingness to assist centers in solving their clients' problems.

Teach Education Classes

Volunteer to teach an educational class at your local town hall or community center. "Over the years, I have taught a number of classes to both CPAs and attorneys," the MDRT sales professional says. "Most of the time, the classes will have an outline, textbooks, and all the material you will need. Teaching classes for centers is one of the best ways to meet new potential professionals. The mere fact that you are teaching their classes gives you implied status and acceptance as a knowledgeable professional."

Form an Industry Study Group

Sometimes, no matter how well-educated you think you are about the products you sell, a lack of knowledge gets in the way of solving your prospect's problem. "I realized I was probably included in this group," he says. "Once I realized that there were subject matters I needed to learn about, I called about twenty of my peers and asked them if they might have the same problem. I suggested that we form a study group and bring in the best resources to bring us up to speed." His study group has been together for three and a half years. "Although technically, we are natural competitors, a bond of trust and respect has evolved that makes it a very enjoyable experience."

Defensive marketing is all about image. It is designed to position you as an expert in your chosen field. The feeling you want to create is one of relief when the center hears you are involved in the case. Imagine the centers saying to one another, "Thank goodness (your name) is involved. Now I won't have to worry about contacting another sales professional for a second opinion. (Your name) knows how to work as part of a team. (Your name) has the product knowledge to do the job right!"

Defensive marketing is not, however, designed to get you referrals per se. Offensive marketing is necessary to get referrals.

Offensive Techniques

Offensive marketing is all about building trusting relationships. These get built one-on-one over time, the same way a friendship evolves. Your goal is to develop the confidence of the centers of influence in your abilities, methods, and motives to do a great job for their clients. You want to produce a win-win for centers and their clients. Always remember the tremendous risk the centers are taking when they refer you. Because you come highly recommended, you are expected to do a good job; therefore, there is very little upside for the center. But if you do a bad job, there is a tremendous amount of downside. Put yourself in their shoes; think about how well you would want to know someone before you referred him or her to your clients. It takes time for a relationship to develop, and that is why referrals are so slow in coming, particularly when you are dealing with relationships that may have taken centers their entire careers to build.

Be advised to pick your most affluent clients carefully, as they take a great deal more time to get close to than others. The same can be said of picking your centers. You will need to spend a great deal of time with them for your relationship to develop and grow.

As one MDRT sales associate says, "Although I have over one thousand centers on my regular mailing and broadcast fax list and twenty thousand who see our advertising monthly, there are only fifty people I see regularly. I make sure we have breakfast or lunch a minimum of once a quarter, ideally every other month. I used to have a complicated system where I categorized my centers into As, Bs, and Cs. As I saw once a quarter, Bs three times a year, and Cs twice a year. Now I see only my best centers four to six times per year. In his book, *The Road Less Traveled,* F. Scott Peck stated that a good indication of what is important to a person is where he spends his time. I want my centers to know they are important to me."

What takes place in these meetings? That depends on how far your relationship has developed. In the beginning, you might want to discuss technical subjects. Later on, the talk can be more about personal things. Over time, if the chemistry is right, your talk will turn into a mutual support session for one another. Your business is not the center of most people's life, as it is your own. With that in mind, in the early stages of the relationship, you should try to become a source for the center. Begin your first meeting with your résumé and your firm's brochure. Find out what kind of practice the center has, and ask how you can be of help. One of the reasons centers may be reluctant to refer someone to you is that they don't know how much your products cost, so leave them rates on your letterhead for your various products and services.

Each time you see your centers, try to have something that you can leave behind with them. In addition, make sure they get your broadcast fax every two weeks, as well as any monthly mailers. And, by all means, don't forget to convey the value of what you sell. Sometimes, sales professionals get caught up in meeting quotas and forget the value of the products and services they are selling. Always think in terms of your products' ability to change lives forever. If you don't call on the prospect, someone else will, someone who may not have your knowledge and products and may not provide as good a service as you would. Who, then, has the most to gain or lose in this transaction? The client is lucky to have someone like you—and you should never forget that.

Ask for help in expanding your business. Another MDRT associate says, "I went through a program with a consultant to develop referrals. We started by reviewing all our clients. We then separated out our best clients. We listed what products or services they bought compared to others. We looked for common character traits, anything that would help us identify why these people were Triple-A clients. We then put together a list on my stationery of the following questions: 'I am expanding my business and I need your help. Who do you know who has an income of (dollar figure) or a net worth of (dollar figure) or more? Who has just purchased or started a new company? Who has personally guaranteed his or her company's bank loans? Who has paid $100,000 or more in income taxes? Who is your favorite client to work with? Who is pleasant and appreciates good service?"

You want to create a picture of a person in your centers' mind. Then tell your centers there are three ways they can introduce you:

1. The ideal way is to call prospects and set up a joint meeting with the three of you.

2. If time doesn't permit that, then have them call prospects and tell them that you "walk on water" and that they need to see you. You can say you need this help to get past "the gatekeepers."

3. If they can't or won't do either, then ask them to tell their prospects about your business, and then you call them.

Finally, sit down with your centers of influence and show them how they can implement the same marketing plan in their practice, reviewing their clients, segregating out the best, developing a similar list, and scheduling a series of meetings telling their clients that they want to discuss three things with them: that they are one of their best clients and they want their feedback on how they can serve them better; that they want to know what it is that the client values most about their relationship or service; that they need their help in expanding their practice. "Who do you know who . . ." You would be amazed at how centers need and want help with marketing.

Last, but not least, bring them clients! I can't send my clients to each of the over fifty centers I see on a regular basis, but I go out of my way to match centers with clients who fit their unique profile.

Cultivating the Confidence of Prospects

When asked about friendship, a leading sales professional in a company that has fostered hundreds of highly successful sales associates says this: "People in this business cannot reach great heights until they have succeeded in cultivating the friendship of others who are in a position to help them in making contacts. Regardless of their ability or experience, their success will ultimately be determined almost entirely by the help that they can get people to give them."

What can you do that will help to make prospects like you? There are many things, but they are all summed up in a statement made some two thousand years ago and now known as the Golden Rule: *Do unto others as you would have others do unto you.*

If you want friends, be friendly. If you want prospects to like you, first be genuinely interested in your prospects—like them and thus be likable.

An able sales professional tells about a sale that he made to a newly arrived stranger in town partly because he took the trouble to write him a letter of welcome (incidentally, a frank one). In commenting on the case, the sales professional says, "I like this person. I like hundreds of people, and I have often thought what a real sales-making advantage an honest liking for our fellow human beings really is. Some of us are naturally more friendly than others, but if there is any one trait, aside from perseverance and hard work, that makes for success in our business, it is liking people. Cultivate it. It is a habit that will grow."

Look for the Good in Prospects

A genuine interest in prospects can be cultivated by looking for the desirable qualities in them and liking them for these qualities. Before going into your prospects' office, house, favorite restaurant, or wherever your interviews take place, make up your mind that you are going to find their best side and that you are going to like them for their favorable qualities, not dislike them for their undesirable ones. Everyone has faults; you have them as well as your prospects: "Judge not that ye be not judged." Don't be unconsciously critical. You are out to sell your products or services, not to improve personalities or make enemies. The first requisites of a good interview are a favorable place and a friendly atmosphere.

In converting strangers to friendly acquaintances and friends, there are no shortcuts or artificial methods that work. Recently, a new family moved into a New England city. A sales professional sent a letter of welcome, mentioning the new addition of a baby to the family. Obviously, there was an ulterior motive, but it was not frankly mentioned. The letter was not sincere; it did not lay all the cards on the table. Later, the sales professional called and talked as if he had known the prospects all their lives. The couple reacted by viewing him as insincere and unduly familiar. Result: the new parents bought—but from the next sales professional who called and to whom this story was told.

Insincere and Too Hasty

A business professional recently was transferred from Missouri to Oregon. A few days after his arrival, he happened to mention to an associate, as they were approaching a restaurant for lunch, that he guessed he needed some more life insurance. Inside, he was introduced to a life insurance sales professional who joined them for lunch. Here was a prospect who was ready to buy and a sales professional ready to sell. But the sales professional did not sell a dime's worth. In telling about it later, the prospect said that the sales professional made a bad impression; he said that he developed right off what he called "an instinctive dislike" for this sales professional. "He was on a first-name basis too soon for me," said this prospective buyer. "Furthermore, I did not like his obsequious truckling and fawning attitude with my associate. He was obviously insincere. He didn't really believe what he was saying."

Moral: First, in crossing the bridge from stranger to friend, don't try to make it in one leap; second, don't say anything unless you mean it. Insincerity is always obvious. If your prospect's daughter has a face that only her mother could love, don't remark on how pretty she is. Talk about her intelligence or her politeness—and only if you mean it. Something nice can be said without resorting to obviously false flattery.

Another MDRT sales professional was asked how he could spend so much time out visiting when he was the second highest sales producer in his company. "That's the way I do good," he said. "I listen to people's troubles and their bragging. I put myself in their shoes. I do a lot of listening and a lot of learning at the same time. They think I'm a swell fellow because I'm always going out of my way a bit to help them or their friends. Doing a favor is the best way I know of to make friends, and friends mean business. At first, I had to do these things consciously; now, it's second nature."

Unselfish Thoughts

The basis of getting people to like you is essentially unselfishness and thoughtfulness. Have you ever noticed how many successful people, in business letters or conversation, throw in a personal note, a sentence or two about hobbies or achievements or family or friends? People like it if they recognize that you are sincere. But don't be like the person who asks you how your wife is and you just have a chance to slip in the answer before he or she is off on another unrelated subject. You recognize that such people ask about your wife or child or father not because they *want* to know how he or she is but because they want you to *think* that they are interested in his or her welfare. There may be only a small difference or no difference in the words used, but there is tremendous difference in the results. The difference between success and failure, just like the difference between sanity and insanity, can be very slight. But a little thing can tip the scales in your favor. A little difference can be a vital difference.

Having a pleasant word for the elevator person is a little thing, but perhaps this person will say something that will help you sell the boss. Smiling at the receptionist is a little thing, too, but it is a big thing if it helps you get in and make a sale. One sales professional says, "A cheery word always seems to bounce back." Another says, "Always be courteous to everybody. More than one sales professional has been made because someone's secretary was impressed with a sales professional's courtesy and deference." Again, thoughtfulness and unselfishness!

The Prospect's Goodwill Means Business

A sales professional who was recently made assistant to the head of a department at his company's home office gives considerable credit for his sales success to his belief that it is better to have people's goodwill than their business. "If you have people's goodwill," he says, "you can get business *from* them or *through* them." He tells about calling on a manufacturing executive several years ago in a small city about fifteen miles from his company's city. The friend-in-the-business excuse stopped him this time, though he had some good answers. It turned out later that the brother of the concern's president was a sales professional and had the prospect's concerns well in hand. The conversation turned (purposefully) to the prospect's business. They become friendly, and the sales professional called on him nearly every time he was in town. He never sold him his product, but, having his goodwill, it was not long before he secured personalized introductions that brought him many times the business he could have secured under the best of conditions from this one prospect.

Another sales professional tells about an acquaintance who had a friend who was going to buy her product. The acquaintance resulted from association at a businesswomen's exercise group at the local YMCA. The sales professional was merely acquainted with the woman but had always taken pains to be courteous and thoughtful of her. "Why did this woman give me the tip and tell her friend not to do anything until she had seen me? I am sure," says the sales professional, "that it was because I had gone out of my way to be pleasant to her as I try to be with everyone."

Sincere Interest: The Key to a Likable Personality

One's personality includes personal charm, or the qualities that make people like one. Sincerity arises in the personality from a feeling of deep and authentic interest in other people and is measured by the extent to which one has acquired the habit and skill of influencing other people through interesting and serving them. You were not born with a personality. You acquired one, and it can be changed and improved if you want to change and improve it.

In his excellent book on personality building, *The Return to Religion,* Henry C. Link makes the point that an improvement in one's skill in getting along with people can only be acquired through practice, not by self-analysis or introspection. "Analyze yourself to find your weak points—certainly—but don't expect to improve your personality by reading books alone," Link writes. "The only way is by doing things that involve other people: going to church, being active in organizations, playing bridge, dancing, selling your product or service." Such activities require paying attention to other people and their interests—discipline in unselfish social habits—which Link regards as synonymous with what he calls the unselfish extrovert type of personality:

> The introverts avoid meeting people, evade obligations of clubs and committees, perhaps think of good deeds but do none. They are self-centered, selfish and perhaps afraid of making mistakes and embarrassing themselves. The extroverts may be afraid, too, but make the sacrifice and by their mistakes and suffering ultimately achieve skill and confidence. Personality is the result of sacrifice and self-discipline—just like most worthwhile things.
>
> From a psychological viewpoint, all friendship involves an artificial process, namely the process of subordinating one's own interests and inclinations to those of others. People who have acquired the art of friendship no longer think of it as artificial. For them it is natural, or second nature, to say and do the things that please others. Indeed, they may even think that they are pleasing themselves, rather than their friends. They are, because to give pleasure to others has come to be their own first principle of enjoyment.

The Sales Professional Who Sold Coolidge

When Calvin Coolidge was president and living at the White House, he bought a product from a sales professional whom he had never met. The sales professional was going to be introduced by a friend who was a colonel in the administration, but the colonel was unexpectedly engaged when the sales professional arrived in town, so he sold himself into the White House. The president liked him and the conversation was pleasant. The product was brought up in a few words, and President Coolidge said yes in his laconic way. A while back, a consulting psychologist, Maude S. Nuttall, wrote a book titled *Gold Book of Life Insurance Selling,* describing this sales professional's personality after having met him at a Washington dinner party. Here is a digest of her estimate:

> He dominated the conversation because he was so interesting that the others wanted him to talk. But he was a good listener and urged some of the others who had traveled widely to tell about their journeys. He had a smile that was easy to remember afterwards. A self-made man with a limited formal education, he was unassuming, natural, and unaffected in his manner and way of talking, though the others at the dinner were persons with unusual education and travel experience. He showed an almost childlike interest in what he was hearing. He made others feel that what they were saying was of extreme importance. His lack of self-consciousness put others at their ease. Though his humor was sparkling, he didn't tell any jokes at the expense of others. Thus no one present was chilled by the thought that they might be victims of his wit. He remembered names; he made it his business. He showed a marked vitality and enthusiasm. His hobby being politics he had a common interest with a number of those at the table. Everything about him won confidence.

Winning the confidence and friendliness of other people is developed through conscious and unselfish effort. Go to church and make it known that you want to help with activities. Lend someone a book. If you collect stamps, meet other stamp collectors. If you are interested in local history, join the historical society. Perhaps improve your poise and speech by joining a dramatic society. Congratulate people on their promotions and other achievements. Help with charity and fund drives. When you drive your car, be considerate of other drivers and of your passengers. But don't forget: it's easier to be selfish until these qualities that people like have become habitual with you. Then, it will be easier to be unselfish.

Expose Yourself to People

Volunteer activity can be overdone, of course, if it is made an end instead of a means to an end. But its value can be proved. Years back, LIMRA International developed a rating plan for use in selecting life insurance sales professionals. It is based on study of the personal histories of over ten thousand full-time sales professionals. The ten most significant personal history items were selected, and a plan for assigning scores to each of them was scientifically worked out. One of the items is current membership in religious, business, political, fraternal, social, and military organizations or clubs or lodges. The score for membership in one organization is 3; for two organizations, 4; for three, 8; and for four or more, 11. Not only does active membership in organizations provide a valuable means of favorable contact with prospective clients, but a person who is a member of several organizations is generally the kind of person who either likes to meet people or wants to learn to like to meet people, and who will not be averse to making contacts, which are so necessary in the selling profession.

Although the likelihood of sales professionals being successful is increased by belonging to a number of organizations, the people who also hold office or have held office in the prior five years in any of the organizations to which they belong are still more likely to succeed. The score for no offices held is 4; for offices in one organization, 7; and for offices in two or more organizations, 13.

Sales professionals who get around among people spend less time in the activities of thinking, reasoning, and analyzing that may lead to rationalizing personality faults, and more time in action, in doing, in the practice of those things that develop habitual and unconscious skill in gaining the liking of people. Furthermore, the people who get around discover selling situations that are the meat and drink of their business. Moral: Keep in circulation.

Recently, a sales professional sat on a jury. A less imaginative sales professional might have tried to be excused, but this one, within a short time after the case was concluded, sold three members of the jury, and although he didn't sell the lawyer for the defendant, who was acquitted, he made such a good impression on him that it led to selling four of his friends.

Getting Means Giving

Personality: the habit and skill of being interesting and serving other people. A sales professional in the Midwest occasionally analyzes the insurance estates of uninsurables. He has no direct hope of making any commissions, but because he takes the trouble, usually finding ways to increase the amount of insurance or its potential value, he earns the unending thanks of these people. They are voluble in their praise of him and he has built up some fine centers of influence among them.

A lawyer once told a well-known sales professional, who related the story in his memoirs, that he was uninsurable and could not buy more life insurance. The sales professional replied that he wanted to build goodwill and would be glad to give him his programming service, which included a record book and leather folder for his contracts. The lawyer was so pleased when everything was concluded with option settlements in order, children named as contingent beneficiaries, and so on, that he showed his law partner what had been done for him. His partner wanted the service too, and bought additional life insurance. This is how people like to be served. This sales professional has the habit. Call it unselfishness or enlightened self-interest. It doesn't matter; it works either way.

Be Interested in the Prospect's Interests

These stories bring home the point that you can't get unless you give. It's the Golden Rule again. Nor can you interest people unless you become interested in what interests them. Smart sales professionals subordinate their own interests to those of the prospect. If their prospect is interested in the architecture of igloos, they are too. This may seem artificial, but with practice, it will become natural.

To interest people, be prepared on a wide front. Have interest in things: automobiles, boats, books, computers. Have interest in ideas: social, economic, and political. Enlarge your knowledge and sphere of interest so that you can interest many kinds of people.

One of the best ways to do this, in addition to your personal contacts, is to read things comparable to the *New York Times* Sunday *Book Review* section and the *Reader's Digest*. It is a frightful commentary on modern life that you have to read reviews of books instead of the books themselves, and digests of magazine articles rather than the originals, but sales professionals must catch the tempo of the times and adjust to it, just as the *Reader's Digest* has.

One reason Theodore Roosevelt was so much liked by people meeting him was his habit of subordinating his own interests. He drew people out of their shells by finding their interests and then, because he was prepared on a wide front, he could be interesting to them by conversing about their interests.

Be Friendly and Cheerful

Emphasize the positive aspects of personality. Be friendly and cheerful. That is what people want and will pay to get. Smile. Dale Carnegie, in his popular book *How to Win Friends,* tells about an able sales professional who attributes much of his success to one of those great big natural smiles that disarm resistance. Just before entering a prospect's office, he thinks of the many things he has to be thankful for and enters the room with the smile just vanishing from his face.

Everyone has observed the close relation between our thoughts and our bodies. If we are angry enough, we get red; if we are happy enough, we exude it. We become what we think, and it behooves sales professionals and strategists to keep their thoughts where they will do the most good and the least harm.

Many years ago, in his book, *Sign Here,* Bert Nelson described an interesting case. As Nelson was leaving a prospect's office, he noticed a nice looking young man seated outside the manager's office. "I smiled as I passed him and he smiled back as though amused. We talked together for a little while and I asked him if he would lunch with me. He did so and I returned to his office with him and told him more about my product—more than he had ever heard before, so he said. At any rate he purchased the product after telling me how much more money he could save each year."

This sale led to many other sales, so it is no wonder that Nelson says "Optimism is a killer of fear and a smile will get under the thickest skin. There is a smile inside of every prospect and your own smile will bring it out. Every time you smile you make life a little brighter both for yourself and the other person." A good smile includes a twinkle in the eye. It is not the artificial facial contortion that you sometimes see turned on and off like a faucet.

People like a cheerful, positive attitude. With some people, everything is negative; nothing is ever right. If business happens to be poor with you when someone asks "How's business?" don't admit it or talk about it. During the latest period of depression, a sales professional asked about the state of his business replied, "Fine, I'm busy as the devil!" A person like that is refreshing.

Prospects Envy Enthusiasm

One of the best definitions of enthusiasm is in Paul W. Ivey's textbook on selling, *Successful Salesmanship:* "Enthusiasm is a spirit that animates the whole body (face, voice, and actions) and makes an attractive and convincing sales professional out of an assortment of dead flesh and bones." Here is another good definition: "Enthusiasm is getting on fire about your business." If you have lots of enthusiasm, don't try to keep it under control. Don't be self-conscious about showing it. Open up! People will envy you and like you for it.

If you do not have much enthusiasm, remember that the best way to develop it is to know your business and be sincere enough to put yourself in your prospects' shoes and feel for yourself what your service can do for them and their families. The value of sincerity for its own sake in getting people to like us has already been discussed.

Be Confident, Not Timid

Be self-confident and forceful, never timid. Timidity puts one on the defensive immediately, and though prospects may try to be extra courteous out of sympathy, their courtesy consists of diplomatic and early easing out of the office. Toughness and other forms of resistance in prospects can be looked on as a veneer covering what is probably the real article underneath. Your job is to get prospects relaxed and out of their shells by being different, by being interesting to them—as is their business, and as is their family when they get home at night. The first step is to be confident, not timid.

As important as personal appearance may be, the best way to become confident is to know that you can be of real service to prospects. This presupposes that you know what your prospects' needs are. As success grows, sales professionals become more confident and then, if they wish, are in a better position to approach people without having secured prior information. Fear is wholly mental and it is also natural. Everyone must learn to overcome it. This takes practice. Inspirational reading is often a great help.

Be Yourself

Another personality characteristic worth cultivation is naturalness. At a sales convention some years ago, a New York City sales professional described how he got his first practical lesson in being natural. As he related, he had taken a sales training course in which he had learned that a good way to get past the administrative assistant is to ask for the prospect in a brusque, businesslike manner. At the same time, the sales professional looks at his or her watch, the implication being that he or she has an appointment with the prospect. The sales professional then turns his or her back on the assistant, further conveying the impression that he or she is not in the market for any further conversation. Quite frequently, the administrative assistant will assume that an appointment has actually been made.

On his first call, the sales professional went through this performance very impressively—but not quite impressively enough, for the assistant, instead of announcing him to the boss, asked him what he wanted to see the boss about. Unable to keep his features frozen any longer, the sales professional wheeled around and with his natural grin said, "If I told you what I'm supposed to tell you, I couldn't keep a straight face, and if I told you what I'm really here for, you wouldn't let me in."

"What is it? You're selling something?" the assistant asked, smiling.

"Yes," the sales professional replied. But the assistant got him in to see the boss just the same. He had a pleasant interview, though no sale resulted. From then on, the young sales professional never attempted any type of sales activity that was not fully natural to him.

Many a potentially good idea has been wrecked in use because it was taken over from a sales professional with one type of personality and put to work intact by a sales professional with another type of personality. The difficulty is that the second user cannot be natural. He or she adopts the idea wholesale instead of adapting it to his or her personality. So—be yourself.

Prospecting through Seminars

A seminar is a classic example of "working smarter, not harder" at all stages of the sales process. Prospecting is easier because you send a no-strings-attached invitation to prospects and clients. Those who accept are already interested in the seminar subject. Barriers are eliminated; people who would not ordinarily agree to an interview may be more comfortable and interested in a seminar.

A seminar enables you to reach a large number of people in a short period of time and is an ideal format for presenting the complex problems that sales professionals must solve today. Solutions to individual needs flow logically from concepts presented at the seminar. When you hold a seminar, you enhance your image as a sales professional. Seminars are an excellent way to run through your preapproach and approach activities with a number of people without having to repeat yourself that same number of times.

What purposes can be served through a seminar? Seminars can be presented throughout the sales cycle for:

✓ *Generating leads:* This type of seminar is designed for unqualified prospects and covers more general topics.

✓ *Approaching prospects:* Qualified names with common characteristics allow for a more targeted, specific presentation.

✓ *Presenting specific products:* These seminars can be directed at both qualified prospects and existing clients who have been targeted as having a specific need or interest.

The first step in putting together a seminar is deciding on the market to address. Ideally, seminar attendees should have something in common—occupation, marital/family status, age, income level—that indicates certain product needs.

Two questions you should ask yourself:

1. Is it helpful to present a diverse group of professionals on a seminar panel?

2. Should I develop or prepare written material for my seminars?

The answer to the first question is that a seminar panel should match a concept to appropriate experts. This might mean including several sales professionals who have different areas of expertise. An MDRT sales professional would want to include tax attorneys, accountants, bank trust officers, pension specialists, stockbrokers, and so on. Whatever the complexity of the seminar subject, the panelists should be knowledgeable in their field as well as articulate on the subject and able to communicate in lay terms.

One advantage to having outside panelists is that they will often supply their own list of names for seminar attendees. Panelists from outside the agency or industry can also help convince attendees that the seminar will be informative.

And yes, answering the second question, handouts are important, both so that people have a tangible reminder of the seminar and to stimulate them to meet with you at another time to discuss their individual needs and concerns.

Chapter 5

Markets

The best sales professionals specialize in a specific market. Prospecting among people who have something in common—a profession, club or affiliation, cultural heritage, age group—is much more efficient than prospecting among anybody and everybody. Let's examine the criteria for a market, tips for selecting a market that is right for the salesperson, and field-tested ideas for generating plenty of prospects from it.

When it comes down to it, the marketing process is the ultimate determinant of success in your business. Marketing is the process that puts you and your products and services in front of the competition, the process that attracts those who are qualified and interested in buying from you. Marketing determines whether or not you are successful as a sales associate because it's your first and last chance to form and validate a positive impression of who you are and what you have to offer.

Initially, through your first marketing efforts, you can form a positive image in a prospect's mind if you go about marketing yourself correctly. The first step in the marketing process is one of the most important because it's the effort that will form a first impression in the prospect's mind. If you go about it the right way, the first impression will be a positive one and will lead to a follow-up with the prospect. Follow four basic steps:

1. Identify prospects and be consistent in sending relative and interesting information.

2. Make a good impression: Pinpoint all the positive points about your company, the ones that make you stand above the competition.

3. Give prospects a reason to contact you, something in the marketing effort that is unique and attractive and will initiate the prospect's call.

4. Validate prospects' image: through the follow-up procedure, confirm the first image that the initial marketing effort forms in the prospect's mind by being truthful to the company's claims of products and services offered.

We can see how every step of the production cycle is part of the marketing process. The first step is to initiate and form an image, and each step along the way gives you the opportunity to market yourself and your services again, over and over, by confirming prospects' positive image of you as you follow up with them.

What is your market?

Before you can begin with the marketing process, you must identify your market. There is a way to see more people, and if you see more of the right people, those who have the need and ability to purchase your products, your average commission will go up. There are three markets that you should consider potential hot markets: the emerging, the affluent, and the rich.

Aim your new marketing efforts at the emerging affluent: young people who will shortly become affluent. This market is open to new ideas and will most likely benefit from your services a short way down the road. By targeting before they become affluent, you have a chance of getting to them before the competition. Devise a market plan aimed solely at this market. For younger or less experienced sales associates, market yourself as at the same level agewise and show how you have innovative ways of servicing them. Make yourself appeal to them. For older or more experienced producers, market yourself as just that: you're familiar with the income bracket that your prospects are in and are familiar with the needs they will have as they progress. Show them that you've been around, you've worked with many people in their situation, and can really be of help to them.

Newsletters: Make Them Your Prospecting Ally

Results are what sales professionals desire most. Results are what you strive for when you cultivate ideas from sales conferences, books, and audiotapes. Results are the tools you use to reach more prospects and complete more sales.

But what do results mean to you? Probably the same thing they mean to most sales professionals. Results mean getting appointments when you ask for them. Results mean closing a sale when you ask for the business. Results mean doing business with your prospects on the first or second appointment instead of the second or third. Results mean having your clients continue to buy from you and give you referrals to boot.

But what does all this have to do with client newsletters? Client newsletters are a way of keeping in touch with your clients and prospects in a nonthreatening way. Why is nonthreatening important? Because if you become too intrusive in your selling practices, prospects and clients may view you as an annoyance, not someone who provides a service.

That's where newsletters come in. Newsletters give you a legitimate reason to call and a starting point for your conversations. They make an excellent complimentary gift that you can give to your clients' friends to introduce yourself. They remind people what a professional you really are. They tell your readers that you're there to serve them, that you're in the business to stay, that you understand their needs, and that you care enough to make an investment in your relationship with them.

How does one know for sure they work? Ask many top MDRT sales professionals and they will tell you about how newsletters have opened many new prospecting avenues. But newsletters won't do your selling for you. They just make your job easier—easier to get the first appointment with a prospect, easier to close a client on one appointment instead of two, easier to manage your time by eliminating the need to make personal contact every time you want to be in touch with your clients and prospects.

A newsletter is a tool. And successful people use tools effectively. To do that, you have to have a goal in mind, you have to make the commitment to a strategy, you have to develop a plan, and you have to work your plan.

Make a Commitment

If you really believe that newsletters are going to help you in your business, then make your commitment. Making commitments is not new to you. You've already made the commitment to be there when your clients need you. You've already made a commitment to provide quality service at all times, and to practice effective time management and resource management.

If you could put a ten-dollar bill down every time you wanted to get an appointment with a prospect, and know that that ten-dollar bill would make the difference between getting the appointment or not, would you do it? Of course you would. That's what one MDRT professional does. He figures that if a prospect is worth a ten-dollar investment, he'll put that prospect on his newsletter mailing list. And since he began integrating newsletters into his way of doing business, his appointment ratio has gone from two out of ten to two out of three. Not bad.

By putting a few dollars a year into a newsletter for each of your prospects, you create a form of insurance, knowing that you'll increase your chances to be successful when you make contact with the people with whom you want to do business.

Develop a Plan

Once you've made your commitment, you have to work out an integrated plan of action. One simple way to develop a plan is to ask yourself who, what, when, why, where, and how. Let's start with *why*.

Why would you want to use a newsletter in your business? One good reason is that newsletters match the commitments you've already made in your profession. They allow you to be there when your clients need information about things that are important to their future. They represent you and your industry in a professional way, and they will help you achieve excellent sales results.

Your primary objective may be to keep the clients you worked so hard to get, to build client portfolios instead of just selling products, to generate more referred leads, to improve results from prospecting, or to increase awareness of yourself as a professional.

The results can be more business from more clients, better quality business, better sales averages, goodwill, and an image that you're proud of. At any level of achievement, with the growing responsibility you take on by building your client base, a sufficient reason to send newsletters is simply to provide the service you promised in the first place. That's how many MDRT sales professionals see it, and they use their client newsletters to keep in touch, even if they don't bring business immediately.

Now that you've answered why, write it down. In fact, write your whole plan down, because making a commitment and putting your goals and plan in writing is the difference between reading this and thinking about it and actually doing it.

The next question is to *whom* are you going to send your newsletters? Research shows that your three best prospect groups are your existing clients, referrals from clients and centers of influence, and prospects in a target group with whom you'd like to do business. Let's deal with each group in turn.

The first people to consider are your current clients. The biggest reason that clients leave you is because they "never hear from you anymore." So you need a way to keep in touch with them when there is no time to call on them in person. By sending them a regular newsletter, you will keep in touch, they will appreciate you, and they'll give their loyalty in return. You can still send out birthday and anniversary cards, product updates, or sales brochures, but your newsletter can be the regular contact that leaves your clients feeling you're always there when they need you.

Referred leads are your second target group and many sales professionals have found a simple success formula that helps them get all the referred leads they'll ever need. This will be addressed later. The difference between a referred lead and a cold prospect is simply this: referred leads have been introduced to you (either directly or indirectly) by someone of influence in their lives. If every prospect could be a referred lead, you'd be one step ahead of the game. But sometimes, there are prospects with whom you want to do business but you have no way of getting to know them other than taking the initiative to introduce yourself. So, when you have to make the first move, newsletters are a great way to introduce yourself. They are a nonintimidating door opener and give you a good springboard to call and talk about ideas that might be of interest to your prospect.

Often, the unstated objection when you talk to referred leads and targeted prospects for the first time is, "But I don't know you. How do I know I can trust you?" This is particularly true for financial matters. Have you ever noticed that people seem more willing to talk about the intimate details of their sex lives than to let you know that they can't even balance their checkbooks! The sad part is, they'd risk their entire financial future because they're afraid to let anyone know that they don't already have it under control.

How do you overcome this resistance? Your newsletter lets them know that you are knowledgeable and that you're here to stay, and it gives them an easy way to talk about financial matters without embarrassment. Here's the approach to take with them: Call first and identify with prospects, using the things you already know about them to establish a link. Then get some easy yeses by asking if it's all right to send the newsletter and to call and get their opinion on it. When you follow up, use the newsletter to start the discussion on matters of importance to them, so you can get an appointment on that first attempt. Here's an example of how that might work:

> Hello (prospect's name), (your name) here. Don Swanson tells me you run a hardware store and you've expanded recently. Wow! You know, I have a growing business too, helping my clients with their needs with the products I sell. I send them my newsletter to keep them informed of things that might affect their future. I'd like to send you a copy so you can see the kind of services I offer. Fair enough? Great. I'll call you in about a week to see if there's anything that catches your interest, then we can get together if you like to talk about how it might apply to you. What's the best time to reach you? Tuesday or Wednesday?

It's common knowledge that referred leads are a good source of prospects, but where do you get these leads? First, leads come from clients; that is, if your clients are happy with your service, if you ask for referrals then you can receive them. You can get great referrals from centers of influence. Centers of influence are people who influence the decisions of others; they could be accountants, lawyers, doctors, or anyone else who can enhance your reputation in the eyes of those they influence.

There's one common myth about centers of influence that should be shattered, and that is that they expect you to be the smartest in the business. It's just not true. What centers want to know is if they give you a name, will the person come back and thank them? By sending them your newsletter, you let them know how well you serve your clients, and they feel confident about referring people to you. Here's how you might do that: when you first put them on your mailing list, send a cover letter and call them to explain what you're doing, why you're doing it, and what you expect in return:

> Hello (center's name), (your name) calling. I know your clients must be asking advice on other subject matters of you all the time, even though your specialty is legal advice. I've started putting out a newsletter for my clients that's full of information pertaining to the products and services I offer, and I thought you might like to have a few copies around just to give them when they ask. In fact, I'd love it if you'd act as an advisor to the newsletter, and just let me know the kinds of subjects you get asked about so that I can write about them in the newsletter. I'll send a copy over to you, and I'll just give you a call next week and see if you have any suggestions and then, if you wish, I can arrange for a few extra copies for your reception area. Terrific. I'll call you next Tuesday.

When you follow up with a visit or a call, centers will appreciate the strokes you give them by asking for their advice. They'll be impressed by the extra service you provide your clients, and they may even distribute copies of your newsletter, if you ask. In fact, all you have to do is ask.

Now you know to whom to send your newsletters: clients, prospects, centers of influence. But where do you want them to be received: at home, at the office, or both? You might address your newsletter to your client and his or her spouse at home. This reinforces your prospect's decision to do business with you. And behind every prospect is a second decision maker who can make or break your relationship with the prospect, and who represents another potential prospect with an entirely different network of contacts.

On the other hand, the office might be appropriate because that's where your prospect might feel more comfortable talking business. Or perhaps your prospect is a center of influence and can distribute your newsletter to associates, giving you more referred business.

Once you know who and where, you have to decide when to send your newsletter. The answer is frequently and consistently, because you want your prospects and clients to think about you when they are ready to make a decision, and that could happen anytime. If you could know when significant events happen in their lives, you'd be there to celebrate a raise or an inheritance, or you'd be there to sympathize in the death of a friend. You can't be there all the time, at least not in person. But you can be there with your newsletter.

A newsletter is something of value to your readers and is likely to be saved from issue to issue. In many cases, it will be left on display on a coffee table or a desk. Picture this: A competitor gets in to meet with one of your prospects or clients to present a sales proposal. The client has your newsletter right there on the desk and says, "Listen, I'll tell you what, I'll call my friend, and see if he or she can offer me a better package. If he or she can't, we'll go ahead. Is that all right with you?" And then your phone rings. Your newsletter lets you compete with anyone anytime, because you're always right there.

How often should you be publishing your newsletter? Well, frequently enough for your clients to feel that your newsletter is a continuing service, but not so often that they start throwing it away because they don't have time to read it. Unless you're in a business where you have to give updates on a weekly or monthly basis, most MDRT sales professionals who produce personal newsletters find that a bimonthly publication serves the purpose well. Quarterly doesn't allow clients to believe that it is a regular service, but bimonthly makes them appreciate it enough to miss it if you stop sending it.

There's one other *when* question, and that is, When in the sales process do you use newsletters? You can use them to introduce yourself, you can use them to begin the fact-finding and needs-analysis process, or you can use them to bridge the gap between sale and delivery of the product. Then you can send newsletters as a reminder that you're always there to help; it is a permanent part of your service to your clients.

Now that you've decided to whom to send your newsletter, it's important to know what to say. To answer this, you have to go back to your goals. If one of your goals is simply to inform your clients about the products you sell, then a newsletter is not the best way to do that. It doesn't take long for a reader to realize that it's a sales pitch and not an information service. So keep the content generic, make it unbiased, don't talk about the product. Instead, give your readers some ideas about planning and time management, and remind them throughout the year of things they should be considering to keep their personal plans on track. It's okay to include a brochure in the same envelope, but keep the two functions separate.

Rather than target your newsletter to one specific group, it's often a good idea to publish a cross-section of articles. After all, among your target group you have a range of different personalities and professions, and each reader is a whole person with a family life, a business life, and a social life, with the need to save, plan, invest, and take care of loved ones. So a variety of articles in your newsletter will ensure that no matter who reads it, they'll gain something from it and find something they could pass on to someone they know. One MDRT associate has an interesting perspective on content. He targets the business market, and he finds that businesspeople don't necessarily want in-depth information about everything. He says they really appreciate easy-to-read, bite-sized chunks of information. That's what he gives them with his newsletters. And they call him when they need more information. How about that? They call him when they need more information. That's how newsletters can create a unique contact with your clients.

What should you include when you send out the newsletter? A cover letter should let your readers know what you're doing, why you're doing it, and what you expect in return. Make sure you tell them whether they can expect regular copies or whether this is a sample you want to discuss with them before you go further. Never imply a commitment if you aren't ready to follow through. You can also include sales brochures, invitations to seminars, or annual review reports.

And don't forget to include some sort of feedback mechanism. Along with your phone number, which you should always include, a business reply card or a return letter and envelope can be very helpful in getting feedback, such as ideas for articles, names of people to send a copy to, suggestions about your service, or even changes of address.

Now, there's a big question to deal with, and that is, What should you invest in a newsletter? Aside from the time and personal resources, you have to figure out how much money to invest in the program. Successful businesspeople budget 5 percent of their anticipated earnings for marketing and advertising. That means, if you're planning to earn $200,000 this year, you should plan to invest $10,000 in advertising and sales promotion.

If you're going to make newsletters the centerpiece of your marketing plan, at least half of that budget should go toward newsletters, because they are a proven method of marketing yourself to those who are most important to you. Some MDRT associates have dropped all other forms of advertising since they started using newsletters because they find the return to be the best value they can get for their advertising dollar.

Finally, the hows. How are you going to produce this newsletter? How are you going to use it? How are you going to track your results? Let's first look at production.

There are three options for producing your newsletter: do it yourself, obtain one from your sponsoring company or one of the companies whose products you sell, or use a newsletter published by an outside publisher, personalized with your own name and photo.

If you choose to produce it yourself, for example, on your personal computer, this is the ultimate in personalization. You can talk directly to your readers and communicate your personal philosophy about the business. But you have to consider what your time is worth and what you do best. You'll have to gather information, write articles, produce graphics, meet deadlines, and make sure the newsletter comes together on time every issue. Although people don't always appreciate the things you do for them, they do notice if you aren't keeping up with your commitments.

If you choose to use your sponsoring company's newsletter, you'll gain a degree of professionalism. But, you may give up personalization and you may find your readers believe it to be biased because it has the company's name on it. It's important to balance the ease of producing a newsletter through your sponsoring company with the image you're trying to project.

The third way is to use an outside newsletter service, especially if it is one that can be personalized. That way, you share the cost of professional writers, designers, and printers with other users, and you're able to delegate the overall publishing responsibility. It may cost you a bit more than the other two options and you may have little or no control over the content. But if you value your time and expertise, you'll stick to what you're good at doing and delegate.

Choose your publisher carefully. First, ask for some back is-sues to determine the appropriateness of content to your target group. Second, find out how you can participate in determining future content. Third, find out what guarantees there are if it turns out the newsletter is not what you expected. Fourth, ask what support is available to help you use your newsletters effec-tively. And finally, ask how much the service costs. Whether you produce them yourself or buy them outside, you'll find that the larger the numbers, the lower the cost per copy.

Whichever option you choose, make sure you read your newsletter before you send it. If you produce it yourself, proof-read it carefully. The last thing you want is to leave an impression that your business practice is less than the best, just because of a few typos. If someone else is doing your publishing, never claim that you wrote the newsletter, but instead tell your clients that you contribute to the editorial board. Then make it a point to work with your publisher to produce the kind of newsletter you want.

Once you have production underway, develop your mailing list. At first, you may be in doubt as to whom to include. A good policy is to separate your prospective recipients into two groups. The first group is composed of people who should receive your newsletter for life: your top clients, family members, friends, centers of influence. The second group is people who will re-ceive just a few issues before you decide whether to put them on your permanent list. You'll want to separate these groups to avoid implying a commitment that you're not willing to keep. So, for the second group, let them know they'll be receiving the news-letter for a limited time or purpose, and let them know what they can do to become permanent recipients. One of the worst things you can do is to begin sending a newsletter to people and then cut them off without their knowing why.

In addition to the mailing list, allow for handout copies and back issues you can give to people in the future. Set up a system for cleaning your list regularly. Some sales professionals are concerned about the cost of extra postage to keep people on the list when they're not hot prospects. One MDRT associate's policy is: Once you put people's names on your list, leave them there even if they say they're not ready to do business right away. Experience has proven for this sales professional that enough of them come around to make it worth the investment.

If you prefer to send newsletters only to people who can bring you business within a reasonable time, then a tracking system should be used. It's been important for you in your business to know what works and to keep track of results on different techniques you've tried. Here's a simple way to do it with newsletters: Every time you take a note down from a prospect or client, it's usually scratched on the first piece of paper you find and later transferred to a more permanent file. Instead of throwing those notes away, set up a binder where you keep track of your mailing lists, and put an envelope in the back. Stick the notes in the envelope, and when you periodically review results, you'll be able to see how many referred names you've gotten, the new business you've written, or appointments you made that you wouldn't have without the newsletter. You can then determine which techniques to continue and which to change.

Simple Success Formula

Now it's time to introduce a simple success formula that can help you get all the referred business you desire. Let's assume you're sending out five hundred copies of every issue. First, set aside one afternoon a month; if you're in a really active marketing stage, you can make that once or twice a week. Select 10 percent of your list and phone them. If you can't reach someone, don't worry about it, just leave a very specific message about a desire for feedback on the newsletter. Of the ones you reach, ask these three key questions:

1. *Which articles appealed to you the most?* Prompt them. They may not have the newsletter in front of them when you call, and you want to make it easy for them to discuss it with you.

2. *What articles would you like to see in the newsletter?* Prompt them again, this time based on what you know about their product needs but haven't been able to discuss with them yet.

3. *Who do you know who would appreciate receiving a copy of this newsletter?* This is your chance to get all the referrals you'll ever want; you can qualify them later.

Here's a typical call:

Hello, (your name) here, just calling up about the newsletter I sent you. I was wondering which of the articles you found to be of interest? Oh really? I hope that gave you some good tips. The last time we talked, you were thinking about starting your own business. Have you made the big commitment yet? Great, so you'll be looking in the newsletter for information that can help you with that effort. You know, I have a lot of that information right here at the office. Why don't we get together sometime early next week and I can share some of that with you? Which would be better, Tuesday or Wednesday for breakfast? Great. I'm glad you're really getting value out of the newsletter. There must be a lot of other people you know who'd appreciate a copy. What about the fellow you were working on that special project with? What was his name again?

When you call back to confirm the appointment, you can use the information casually gathered in your newsletter conversation to begin the fact-finding and needs-analysis process, and create an opportunity to close on the first appointment.

When you call clients and ask the three questions, they feel that you care about them. You not only send them the newsletter, but you're also interested in their opinion about it. Also, you have an opportunity to get more referrals. Further, you make it easy for your clients and prospects to discuss what's on their minds.

Remember the first time you talked with a client and the resistance that was there at the beginning? When you finally broke through and made it easy for the client to discuss financial matters with you, you could tell he or she really appreciated you. That's the kind of response you can get by using newsletters to follow up appointments.

Now we've got the whole plan in order: the who, what, when, why, where, and how. The next step is to work your plan. One of the things we've discovered is that many agents get excited about newsletters but then don't follow through. You can't just send them out in a mass mailing and hope people will call you or drop into your office. Yes, you're looking for results. And results mean an idea, plus the commitment and the action to make it a reality. Stay creative while you're putting your plan into action, and keep your eyes open for extra opportunities to turn your newsletters into results. Results! Results! Results!

Here are a few examples:

Use the newsletter to get speaking engagements. Select a few organizations with members you want as clients and contact the person in charge. Put a biography together and send it along with your newsletter and a cover letter outlining the talks you do and how long they take. Later, follow up with a phone call. Remember that most associations have no budget for speakers, so if you tell them you'll do it on a complementary basis in exchange for people's names, they'd be glad to have you there.

Introduce yourself through your newsletter. That way your prospects will feel they know you when you call. And remember, if your goal is to sell a million dollars' worth of your products, send your newsletter to someone who is capable of giving you that much business.

Make it personal. A handwritten note can increase your return. A handwritten envelope is more inviting to open. Try to delegate things like making labels, stuffing, or hand-writing addresses, but take those few important seconds that only you can give to include your signature or a note.

Involve your family. Just like your clients who have a second decision maker at home, you have one too, with a completely different network of contacts and, likely, children who could help you with the mailings. One sales associate asked his wife to distribute a handful of newsletters at the bridge club. Normally, club members didn't discuss what their spouses did for a living. This time they did, and he got three new clients as a result.

Remember, your newsletters don't do your selling for you, they just make it easier. It's up to you to turn your newsletter investment into bottom-line results. So follow up—persist.

Projecting a Powerful and Confidence-Building Image

In the three seconds it takes to walk into a room and extend your hand to potential clients for the first time, prospects have sized you up and made irreversible judgments about you. Before you even open your mouth to say a worthwhile word, your prospects have captured the essence of who you are by the countless signals you send out. The twinkle in your eye, the expression on your face, the outfit you're wearing, the way you sound—all of these influence your prospects' reactions. Clearly, those judgments aren't based on your character. Rather, it's an instinctive response to your power image.

How much does your image determine someone's reaction to you? Advertising agencies and behavioral scientists don't agree on the exact percentages, but their studies indicate that looks influence our judgments. Appearance accounts for well over 60 percent of the impression you make; your voice and the content of your conversation account for less than 40 percent. So what goes through your prospects' mind as they try to decide whether to deal with you?

Instantly, they can decide if you appear to be of comparable social standing. If they like what they see, they'll tolerate you and continue to be attentive and listen to your pitch. If you seem to be of higher social standing, they will admire you or scrutinize you further to assess your power. Prospects want to determine what can be gained by associating with you. If you appear to be of a lower social standing, you're insignificant in their scheme of things and you'll be kept at a distance. These conclusions apply everywhere, from powerful business meetings to social events.

Barbara Walters tested this theory on her television show *20/20*. Two actors simulated a stressful situation; strangers readily came forward to help the more attractive, clean-cut gent, but they ignored the pleas of the scruffy one. The message is obvious: If you want a positive reaction to your image, polish your act.

Demeanor, manners, wardrobe, and voice—all are three-second showstoppers that reveal where you're coming from and either capture prospects' interest in your message or short-circuit their attention before anything significant happens.

The Choice Is Yours

You can control the impression you make at any level, if you're flexible enough to tune in to other levels of power. Opportunities are better for those sales professionals who have the wisdom to modify their behavior in order to move easily in any social tier. The art of making people comfortable is the ability to be gracious in any setting and put other people at ease.

You can opt to enhance your savoir faire to soar with the eagles or you can opt to remain unchanged. Either way, don't limit yourself by deciding that you must stay true to your own set of values. Values aren't virtues or morals, and values do change. To be obstinate by digging in your heels about modifying your demeanor will limit your opportunities and force you to function in only one stratum of power.

"Take me as I am" is a risky choice because sophisticated prospects who move in wider circles are more broad-minded. Their experiences have enriched their perspectives on life. As they see more of the world, they become less tolerant of narrow values and adherence to one group's restrictions. They don't give a damn about how things are done in Des Moines because they function at levels higher than provincial plains.

Power brokers harmonize with their own circle of friends. The challenge is for you to learn to synchronize your style with theirs to be accepted into those circles. Changing your manner of delivery to accommodate a targeted audience is as easy as buying a new suit. Transform your appearance, but never forsake your integrity. A red flag will go up if there's any perception of a flaw in your character. We all know that an Armani suit will never conceal Mike Milken's imperfections.

Projecting a more powerful image sounds provocative, especially if it affects your bottom line. The trick is to pull it off without making a faux pas or appearing gauche. Slipups seldom happen when you're familiar with the rules of the clan. The nail biting begins when you're in over your head. Don't despair: it's easy to move comfortably in any milieu, once you learn the protocol necessary to open the golden doors. The challenge of becoming more polished is worth the rewards!

Target Your Audience

How do you begin? Marketing experts study the demographics of a targeted audience before trying to promote services or products. By the same token, your potential clients have varying backgrounds, so don't settle on one campaign that you hope will appeal to everyone. The challenge is to figure out how to customize each presentation so it will appeal to your prospects. It has to be relevant to their lifestyles; no one wants to buy an Edsel. The smartest strategy is to take the time to carefully profile each individual you plan to call on before making your first appointment. Make a checklist of the personal dynamics that may affect your prospects' judgment. This technique is not artificial; it's a sincere way to show that you care about their intellectual and emotional needs.

Once prospects recognize that your efforts will benefit them in some way, they'll begin to have confidence in your message. If this approach increases your sales rate, why not customize your persona to accommodate their values system? Empathy is a powerful tool for persuading others.

Following is an overview of the four important categories to use as a guideline to measure potential clients:

✓ Social status or class level.

✓ Cultural and ethnic mores.

✓ Individual style.

✓ Personal temperament.

Within each category are distinctive characteristics that will influence your findings. Each individual has personal values that influence his or her needs and motivations. Their behavior reflects these standards.

Let's break down the first category of *social class* into three class structures.

Affluent

Prospects who are affluent have idiosyncrasies unlike prospects from any other class of people because of their sense of entitlement. Whether or not they are born with a silver spoon in their mouth, they expect to be treated with deference.

- ✓ Respect their time: arrive promptly and leave early.

- ✓ Respect their title and identity: refrain from calling them by their first name until they indicate otherwise by inviting you to become less formal. In some countries, assuming this instant familiarity is considered a major mistake.

- ✓ Praise their business-related accomplishments, never your own.

- ✓ Seek information through indirect statements rather than by aggressive probing. They may ask direct questions, but refrain from doing the same.

- ✓ Never discuss personal topics such as age, income, politics, religion, or domestic tribulations. Certain personal matters are sacrosanct and always off-limits.

- ✓ Never reveal their confidences if you want them to trust you. They'll soon find out if you do.

- ✓ Inquire about their offspring or favorite sporting activities so they can grandstand with you. This gives you an opportunity to assess their moods.

- ✓ If you want to personally speak to affluent prospects on the telephone, call their office early in the morning, at high noon, or after their assistants have gone for the day.

✓ Return their telephone calls within twenty-four hours from wherever you are.

✓ Accept their appointment cancellations or delays with grace.

✓ Be proactive on all projects and attentive on follow-through.

✓ Be considerate of their staff; they're the gatekeepers who let you in.

✓ Dress with respect for their role by wearing stylish clothes of the finest quality. Grooming and personal appearance rank high on their values scale. They won't appreciate a full head of curly locks or a beard.

Middle Class

This includes people from management or middle-class levels who know more about political skills than about protocol. They embody the characteristics of conservatives who never make waves. They feel it is important to belong to community organizations and protect family values.

When you meet with prospects from this social class, they want you to show concern for their personal needs. If you are to bond, your language and demeanor must match theirs. They like being the average person next door, but relish being treated as if they were from a higher class. To make a powerful impression on them, customize your presentation to compliment their psyche, not their persona.

Lower Class

The technicians, support, and service people around the world are project-oriented and require fewer formalities. Their goal is just to get a job done. Financial constraints affect their attitude, so beware of displaying any pomp and circumstance: it will turn them off. Only a meat-and-potatoes presentation will do. Of all of the classes, members of this group are the most narrow-minded and controlled by their peers.

- ✓ Use first names only after suggesting that they call you by yours.
- ✓ Keep the conversation casual before making your presentation.
- ✓ Offer technical information that they can understand.
- ✓ Dress more casually if that's the norm.

Cultural and Ethnic Mores

Regional
Geographical areas around the world draw people seeking similar cultural and ethnic associations. Behavior in coastal or hub cities is influenced by a mix of these ethnic and religious groups. At one time, certain regions drew one particular sect; now, major cities are flavored with a religious mixture of Christians, Jews, Muslims, Hindus, Shintos, and Sikhs—each with their own taboos and restrictions that influence the rituals and time of day when business can be transacted. In cities like New York, San Francisco, Toronto, Montreal, London, Paris, and Rome, where cultural activities flourish, the intelligentsia and social sophisticates influence the mores.

It is vital to understand regional idiosyncrasies. As an example, in certain sections of the United States, historical pride dictates behavioral eccentricities. You will go a long way if you make an impression on well-educated, Calvinistic, parsimonious New Englanders. Leave the bells and whistles behind: all they want are logical reasons explaining why they should invest in your products or services. Once they are convinced, they will refer all of their friends to you.

In the Deep South, natives with little use for an aggressive Northern carpetbagger will consider the prospect of dealing with you only if you charm them by exchanging small talk at a leisurely pace. Most people will be attentive and comprehend your message if it's delivered at approximately 175 words per minute. And remember to give them the opportunity to add comments from time to time. Everyone enjoys participating in a good conversation. It takes time, but if they like your finesse, there's hope of making a sale. If not, the meeting may end on a bittersweet note, with your Southern clients dismissing you by saying, "Bless your heart, you try so hard, but you're a mess!"

Californians are an eclectic lot on the more creative side. Many of them respond well to an imaginative approach, so make a powerful impression by being fashionably dressed, well-groomed, and fit-as-a-fiddle. A healthy attitude and body are key to their lifestyle.

International

Each country takes pride in its heritage and the natives expect to be shown respect for their national traditions. Americans tend to discount the pride felt by citizens of other countries, especially neighboring ones. Canadians are sensitive to this oversight and appreciate being praised for their propriety and high standards. Canadian prospects will respond to a conservative approach served up in a well-mannered way.

Mexicans enjoy the more casual lifestyle that goes with their warmer climate. The pressure to be letter-perfect is less intense at the middle and lower levels where natives believe in their customs and traditional ways. However, the affluent classes are well-traveled elitists who expect to be treated as royally as the Castillians of Spain. Only top-of-the-line presentations will influence them!

To project a powerful image in most of Europe, customize your sales presentation to the upper-class level. Show them deference every step of the way. They are sticklers for punctuality, so plan to arrive on time, never early, and walk in with confidence, wearing your best-looking outfit. You will win favor if you treat them with manners fit for a king.

People abroad follow centuries-old traditions that must be acknowledged before business transactions begin. An understanding of cultural differences and nuances will smooth your way and prevent embarrassing slipups. Bowing, shaking hands, or nodding are ways of greeting strangers. In the United States, sales professionals greet prospects by shaking their hand. Using their right hand, they interlock their palm with their prospect's hand and move their hand into the base of a prospect's thumb. This may not be appropriate in some countries, where it is taboo to be touched.

What is correct in one country may not be so in another. It is recommended that you read Roger E. Axtell's *Do's and Taboos Around the World* for more tips about these differences. He explains the four basic requirements: how to say people's names, eat, dress, and talk.

Names and Status

Everyone takes pride in his or her name, but in some cultures, one's name is less important than one's title. That is the reason for the ritual of immediately presenting a business card that includes pertinent information—no abbreviations, please. This helps the prospect who reads your card determine your level of power, so that you will be introduced to someone of equal stature. When you pass your card, use your right hand, never your left, in Southeast Asia, Africa, and the Middle East (except Israel). And in Japan, present it with both hands, thumbs on the corners of the card, with the type facing the recipient.

Never use a first name without an invitation—it's highly improper. It may happen after you establish a long association, but don't hold your breath. Even staff members address their boss by their last name as a sign of respect. Receptionists treat callers with the same civility, unlike their counterparts in the States, those gum-chewing receptionists who immediately act as if you are a personal friend by calling you by your given name.

Bostonians used to have extreme rules to maintain certain levels of civility. Maybe some of you have heard of the famous toast made there in 1910: "And this is good old Boston, the home of the bean and the cod, where the Lowells talk only to Cabots, and the Cabots talk only to God."

Says one MDRT professional: "Let me offer an example of how strictly people hold to class levels. I recently opened an annual report and was amazed to discover a section on 'Lessons in Japanese Etiquette.' The Aeon Group in Japan, the international conglomerate that owns Talbots, states: 'The mark of a well-educated Japanese is the ability to communicate politely in the appropriate situation. The relative age and social position between the speakers, such as a boss and subordinate, a sales person and customer, or two friends, will indicate the politeness required.' Whoever thought being so polite could be so difficult?"

Hospitality

International companies believe it is important to entertain a guest to establish rapport before beginning a transaction. It's also an excuse to ply you with liquor to loosen your tongue. When dinner begins, you are expected to partake of whatever the host serves, even if it includes raw fish in Japan, bear paw soup in China, escargot in France, and firewater throughout.

Muslims in Arabia and Sikhs in India want to break bread and drink tea with you before they show any interest in your sales presentation. A powerful bond will occur during a meal if you answer their questions with lengthy and flattering answers. A typical conversation may go like this: "How was your flight to my country?" A wise response is, "It was impressive to fly over Saudi Arabia, the cradle of civilization and the home of the Kingdom of Islam, where Mecca is."

You announce to the world your sense of grace when you have good table manners. Victorian heritage is a definite asset in today's boisterous world of rude characters. It is an art form that distinguishes you from others. For those who are unfamiliar with the correct form, Tiffany's book on table manners is highly recommended.

Influential business professionals often escort clients to an exclusive restaurant or club for dinner where guests dine Continental style. The purpose of the meeting is to establish esprit de corps. No one is there for nourishment, so wait until everyone is served before taking a bite of food. Ignore the etiquette books that claim it's all right to begin once the people on either side of you have been served. When you eat, what you eat, and how you eat are important. It's also essential to pace your eating in cadence with your host. Start when the host starts, and stop when the host stops. The host is orchestrating the evening.

The mistakes we make often involve little things our mothers failed to teach us: Keep your lips closed when chewing, and never talk with your mouth full. The appearance of an open mouth is so repugnant to Asians that they cover their mouths as they sip their tea or take bites of food.

It is also distasteful for Asians to see dirt on the sole of anyone's shoes, so they courteously slip their shoes off at the door. In most cases, you will appear more refined and well-grounded if you keep both of your feet flat to the floor. However, if you do cross your legs, raise one leg up far enough to be able to lock it over the other leg so both legs will form one powerful line. Remember to keep both feet parallel, with your toes pointed in the same direction. This rule holds whether you are standing, or sitting with your legs crossed.

Another thing we forget to do is take small, bite-sized pieces of bread before adding butter. We pass the salt without the pepper, when in fact the pair are supposed to be passed as a unit and placed in front of the next person. This ritual comes from the superstition that it's bad luck to hand anyone salt. Asians also find people offensive who sneeze, blow their noses, or yawn during dinner.

The French shudder when they see a person cut across the tip on a wedge of brie instead of cutting at an angle, as if it were a piece of pie. They also dislike any discussion of money and fault people who constantly ask or speak about the cost of things.

Personal Temperament

Your ability to adjust to your potential clients' status and heritage influences your success, but more important is having insight into their personal temperament. Your attempt to project a powerful image will fail if you don't customize your presentation to suit their personalities.

What follows are some of the characteristics that will help you discern which of the four main personality types you may encounter. You can learn more on this subject by reading the works of Carl Jung, the famous psychologist. Perhaps you are familiar with the Myers-Briggs Type Indicator tests based on his theories.

Traditional Thinkers. Talk about the mainstay of society. These prospects make life better for everyone because of their work ethic and high standards. They are conservative by nature and think like robots. Everything in their office is organized, catalogued, and researched, so come into the meeting well prepared.

Sitting in their high-back leather chairs, in an orderly office, they will notice within three seconds every detail of the way you look, from your Ferragamo classic shoes, well-tailored suit, and small-patterned Hermes tie, to your Mont Blanc pen.

Contemporary Intuitors. Be prepared to meet inquisitive perfectionists who don't waste time. You'll lose their attention if you wander on and on. Like Bill Gates, the computer genius, they have a vector mind: a right-brain orientation that goes to the heart of the matter in a flash. Only 10 percent of the population fall into this category, so you're dealing with rare birds.

Their offices will be as reflective as they are, with mirrored walls and a view from large-scale windows that take in the world. Glass-top tables and recessed lighting signal their futuristic taste for new ideas. Nothing old-fashioned or traditional about them. Appeal to their artistic sense by coming to the meeting wearing your Armani suit and Swatch watch.

Realist Sensers. These matter-of-fact egotists take life in stride. They may seem amiable because of their sense of humor, but don't waste their time building your case. They are fickle, competitive, and opportunistic, so get to the point quickly. They are action-oriented and look for short-term personal gain.

If you walk into their office without any previous knowledge about their temperament, take a look around for clues. Sensers fill their walls and bookshelves with personal trophies and memorabilia that remind them of their conquests.

Expect them to wear clothes that are functional and simple in style. To complement their taste, arrive in your neat, shadow-plaid suit from Brooks Brothers or a classic-style knit dress from St. John's. Wear comfortable British walkers or Bass loafers instead of formal lace-ups or patent leather pumps.

Compassionate Feelers. A concern for mankind dominates this type of prospect. Their sensitivity to others is based on their emotional reactions. If they like you, they'll listen to your anecdotes and even share some stories of their own. Just when you think you've persuaded them to sign on the dotted line, they'll tactfully turn the corner and walk away. Greet them with a big smile and a warm handshake because they react more to your feelings than to your clothes, long hair, or beard.

Their offices are a dead giveaway to their style. They're messy and filled with disorderly stacks of papers that they never quite get through because they are so busy delving into human resources matters. They will be wearing something unstructured with soft lines rather than a dress-for-success suit. Appearance is not how you'll be judged. This is one time when it's okay to wear a casual outfit made of a supple fabric, or pants with a sweater set or an unlined blazer. Toss a shawl over one shoulder or tuck a small, colorful pocket square in your tweedy blazer to add a dash of color to your ensemble.

Perpetuating a Powerful Image

If projecting a powerful image sounds like a challenge, it is. Image is not skin deep. You must constantly polish yourself and your environment, just as you have to keep up with polishing the silver, to keep impressions of you favorable. Little things count big to build and maintain your professional reputation.

Make the effort to remain valuable and visible as if you were a company budgeting nearly 15 percent of its annual budget for advertising and promotion to maintain brand recognition. Are you a little tarnished? Do you enhance your own image regularly by paying attention to details like your personal health? Would it be wise to hire a personal trainer to get back in shape? Can you take courses for fun, such as Chinese cooking or bonsai gardening? What about treating yourself to a weekend at a glamorous spa? Or an up-to-date makeover? Will people notice a fashionable change in your hairstyle and glasses?

While you're at it, check out your environment. Are there fresh flowers in the reception room and a rose on your administrative assistant's desk? Does your office need a fresh coat of paint? And what about that stack of papers in the corner? Is it worth a few hours to sort through it?

What about the finer things of life and the small considerations that influence your powerful image? Do you write your thank-you notes by hand on engraved stationery within 24 hours after an occasion? A short note is appropriate on a 4½″ × 6¼″ correspondence card or on a 6″ × 8″ social-size sheet of bonded paper. Don't even consider writing with an inexpensive pen. Buy a good fountain pen because nothing can replace the impression of a handwritten letter penned in dark color ink.

Speaking of writing, are your internal memos easy to read? Do you proofread all documents and spell-check computer-generated letters before sending them to others? Recently, the chairman of a major company asked an associate's opinion about two employees he was considering for promotion. The associate asked to see a sample of their informal memos to help him consider the request. One note was scrawled in pencil on yellow-lined legal-size paper. The other was legibly written in ink on a clean piece of typing paper. Can you guess which candidate impressed the associate more?

Do you answer your telephone with a lilt in your voice, or do you offer a quick hello-I'm-busy tone? When you place a call, do you identify yourself immediately by giving your full name before asking the other party if it's an appropriate time to talk? Answering machines and e-mail are convenient devices designed for those who step away from their desks. Occasionally, we all leave town on business and call back for important messages after regular business hours. Sometimes, you are in a different time zone when your administrative assistant is not in the office. When you call prospects and get their answering machines, do you remember to speak slowly and include your own phone number with your message?

Speaking of manners, are you being considerate of others? When was the last time you treated a favorite client to lunch in your private club or a posh restaurant in gratitude for continued business? Do you occasionally invite spouses or significant others to make it a foursome? Your partner is your deepest admirer, so include him or her from time to time. Everyone will enjoy the event.

At a business meeting or industry event, do you introduce everyone in your immediate circle with consideration for a person of more senior stance? The protocol is easy if you always remember to address the senior person first. For example, "Mr. Jones, may I introduce Anne Smith, who is one of my clients? Anne, this is Bob Jones, the president of our company." In less formal settings, it is correct to begin by using only first names: "Bob, this is Anne Smith, a client of mine. Anne, this is Bob Jones, our president."

The list goes on.

Are you just a big talker, or do you walk the walk by volunteering to help in community service and philanthropic activities? Why not go beyond the norm and get personally involved with your favorite charity? Says one MDRT sales associate:

A few years ago, I was chairperson of a fund-raising drive for the Orthopaedic Hospital in Los Angeles. Afterwards, I formed a guild of volunteers to assist the doctors in putting casts on crippled children. Twenty-five years later, the group is still going strong.

When the Boy Scouts needed career training for teenage members of the Explorer Scouts, I recruited six corporate executives to assist me. To express my gratitude, I proposed them for membership on the Explorer Board. We arranged training meetings for the youngsters with speakers from a variety of industries. When it became obvious that training several thousand youngsters was going to be a monumental task, I invited the Junior League volunteers to step in and design a program to continue the counseling. The following year, I recruited a Pepsi-Cola executive to serve on the board of the Greater New York Council of the Boy Scouts with sixty-five other tycoons of industry. Much to my surprise, I was invited to join the board myself. In 1993, the Scouts honored me with their Leadership Award.

This domino theory can become a reality for you, too. You know how it works: one award or special recognition is given by a reputable organization and another group follows suit. Many fine leaders from major corporations serve on philanthropic committees and community boards. Working for the same cause is an easy way for you to meet them and share a worthwhile experience. At some point, this bonding will become an asset in your professional life. It certainly increases your circle of friends and acquaintances.

The potential to serve on nonprofit boards is within your reach, if you give more than you expect in return. Public service is a valuable way to build an impressive image, and all it takes is one step forward to offer your time as a volunteer. Nothing compares with the satisfying feeling you get from helping other people reach their potential.

Electronic Marketing: An Essential Ingredient for Maximum Exposure

A not-so-funny thing happens to some sales professionals on their way to the marketplace with products and services. After considerable research prior to the unveiling, and following months—if not years—of making sure they are utilizing the right marketing tools, they sometimes feel uncomfortable, as though something is missing. And, when they feel this way, they're usually correct in their assumptions.

What has often been overlooked is the utilization of electronic marketing vehicles that can spell the difference between success and failure. Because of their dynamic nature, such valuable marketing vehicles as CD-ROMs, kiosks, videotape, audio cassettes, and/or television and radio can often deliver and reinforce your message more effectively than print. This is not to suggest, in any way, that print shouldn't always be an integral part of your overall marketing strategy. However, it most definitely is meant to imply that electronic media should never be overlooked, which it sometimes is, and often because of preconceived notions that it is prohibitively expensive. Because companies spend considerable time and resources on research and development, it behooves them to look into electronic media—lest some golden sales opportunities pass them by.

Opportunities

Electronic media technology can—and does—create and enhance relationships. And the goal of sales professionals must now and forever be to create relationships with prospects and clients where they, as sales professionals, are viewed as:

✓ Having an in-depth understanding of the specific market's unique problems.

✓ Experts in assessing issues and providing a broad range and/or highly specialized solutions.

✓ Helpful and professional in educating prospects/customers in their best interest.

But how do sales professionals get an opportunity to demonstrate that they can create the right solutions for their prospects? And how can prospects know it's worth their time to even see sales professionals? Whereas sales professionals absolutely and positively know they have something of value to offer, it's generally not as clear to prospects. They must have an answer to the "What's in it for me?" question.

Here's where interactive media, particularly CD-ROM, can play an especially important role. But first, let's look at how the environment for selling has changed—and why it often seems more difficult to reach today's customer.

The Selling Climate

Prospects have become much more sophisticated. Most prospects in the markets you want to reach have been brought up to one degree or another with TV. And though you might not consider sophistication a result of watching television, it has made a massive impact, in at least two ways, on consumers' expectations of how they will receive information:

✓ Prospects now expect to be entertained if they're receiving information. Everything is a story. Notice, as you undoubtedly have, how products are sold through this medium. Advertising messages are embedded in some type of more or less compelling story. A review of some of the commercials created to run during the Super Bowl would show the length some advertisers have gone to create a story they hoped consumers would remember.

✓ Prospects can pick and choose the messages they want to see with a flick of the remote control. Although this can be attributed to a certain degree of fickleness, it really has evolved as a survival strategy. Everyone is simply bombarded with more information than they can possibly cope with. So, what they see better be relevant and useful to them—which is the power of choice exercised with the remote.

Prospects have multiple priorities and less time, with even less patience to wade through information that is not highly specific to them. The types of consumers that sales professionals want to reach generally do not complain about not having enough to read or not enough to do. And general, one-size-fits-all information just doesn't work anymore. Today's consumers simply do not have the time to figure out why they need what you're selling. They must immediately understand "What's in it for me?"

So, how does interactive media fit these issues? Interactive CD-ROM is perhaps the best example because of its ability to hold video files—in essence, to mimic television. However, until interactive television becomes a reality (and it's currently being tested), CD-ROM adds a dimension that TV cannot: the ability to engage in an interaction, to become involved. And this, of course, is what buyer-seller relationships are based on, and perhaps explains why this medium is rapidly growing in popularity among consumers.

CD-ROM not only allows large amounts of information to be presented in multiple formats—compelling video stories, audio reenforcement, and visually appealing text—but, done correctly, it also allows consumers to choose the level and combination of information that best suits them, plus participate in segments that can deliver information customized specifically for them. This type of interaction starts to create a bond, in no small part because consumers are able essentially to drive the show and get what they need. Who wouldn't want to continue a relationship that starts like that?

How does this kind of tool fit the needs of sales professionals? A CD-ROM, as a lead-generation vehicle, can help sales professionals gain entry into hard-to-reach markets when information of value to the market is presented. As a prime example, a large national insurance company offered a CD-ROM as an informational premium item. Through the use of a series of lifelike episodes, the CD-ROM pictured common emotional issues faced by the target market and allowed prospects to view a range of solutions, from not-so-good, to typical, to good. Viewers could hear a consultant's analysis of each solution, plus access information leading to the next step. The company's utilization of CD-ROMs for the campaign was greeted with enthusiastic response by both the field force and target market, and led to generating many qualified leads for sales professionals.

The program was successful because the target market was able to identify with the emotional issues presented as well as receive information that was of value to them. CD-ROMs can—and do—position sales professionals as credible, knowledgeable, and professional. CD-ROM's ability to reach prospects on emotional levels can help prospects identify for themselves a point of need, making the follow-up discussions with producers more productive. And, as a relationship-building tool, CD-ROM programs simply give sales professionals more opportunities for substantive and continuing dialogue with their clients and prospects.

Impact at the Corporate Office

What does this do for the corporate sales office? As a marketing tool, CD-ROM can deliver a substantial competitive edge, positioning the company and sales staff as partners with a vested interest in the well-being of their clients and prospects. Also, from a corporate office perspective, these vehicles can be of help in managing sales practices by providing consistency of information to both the field and prospects. In addition, from a recruiting standpoint, this level of support can be an extremely attractive draw to high-level sales associates.

A new application for CD-ROMs is seminars. Selling by seminar, a long-time effective strategy of top marketers, becomes even more appealing with the use of CD-ROM technology. Now, more than ever, the presenter and members of the audience can become involved.

The setting isn't a flip-chart of slides, but an environment filled with true interaction provided by a mere tap on the keyboard, with the information and accompanying visual brought back to the screen as often as requested and needed. What you'll inevitably and quickly find within such a presentation is the establishment of immediate dialogue, often followed by rapport between presenter and audience. And, as any experienced marketer can attest, that's the first necessary step leading to sales and an ongoing relationship.

So, what CD-ROMs offer is the unique ability to become involved. They erase the wonderment as to whether clients and prospects have read what you have sent them. What you're sending them is all on the screen, and during sales presentations and within seminar settings, you are there to answer their questions.

CD-ROMs also have the ability to direct large amounts of information into manageable segments. And, because the viewer is able to drive the flow of information at many different levels, the audience is, to understate, no longer passive.

Also, although updates to CD-ROMs, as with other electronic media, are periodically required, most of the investment is up front.

Alternatives

Another form of electronic marketing is kiosk technology. Kiosk is particularly effective in worksite marketing or other environments where it's necessary to reach a large number of people at one time. The information can be furnished through an easy-to-use touch-screen system. For example, employees can use their ID numbers to enter the system and be provided with an incredible amount of information on their current employee benefits, the cost, and their eligibility for other products being offered, plus information on other company benefits. A growing number of companies are using kiosks as a marketing tool. This electronic medium serves as a terrific and complementary visual vehicle to printed material furnished to employers, employees, and/or meeting attendees.

Videotape, another form of electronic marketing, is certainly audience-convenient. And although they may require more commitment from the viewer, videotapes can convey more complex information. They are most useful when benefit-oriented education is required, but can also be used in many stages of a marketing program in conjunction with, or in lieu of, a sales force. Not so incidentally, videotapes generally have medium-budget requirements and production schedules.

Because they usually attract attention, another tool to be considered part of the marketing mix is audiocassettes. They're also easy to produce and use at a time and locale (office, home, or in the car) most convenient to the listener.

Continuing along the electronic marketing trail, there are, and always will be, broadcast television and radio. If your goal is to increase awareness, TV or radio commercials work well and appeal to a broad audience. Such commercials are also highly effective as a direct response medium when coupled with toll-free telephone numbers. TV commercials, as you've undoubtedly heard, come with moderate- to high-budget requirements. Radio, as an alternative, is less expensive to produce and comes with less costly air time.

Finally, mention was made earlier of interactive TV, which is still being tested. Viewers will be able to request detailed information about a product or service during television commercials. Merely by clicking a button on their TV remote control, they'll be able to replace the commercials with the requested data on their screen and browse, request details, and even fill out an application by using an infrared keyboard.

But that's not all. Interactive TV, in its broadest application, will enable viewers to speak to a sales professional from the convenience of their home, office, or wherever they may be.

What about the Web?

You may have noted that mention of the Internet has been absent thus far. It's yet to be seen how effective this medium may prove to be. But what has been discovered so far is that the Internet is currently most effective when used with other media.

As a leading example, a Web site is an ideal locale to gather information on prospects. And those surfing can be given the choice, along with your message, on how they want to receive information from you—whether it be your company's information or from you directly, that is, via the postal service, e-mail, phone, fax, or a personal visit from the company's sales representative.

So, when it comes to electronic marketing, fasten your seat belts. We'll continue to be in for some exciting and, for astute industry marketers, profitable times.

Prospecting and Selling in the Mature Market

Today's aging population cannot be ignored. In fact, research indicates that those prospects age fifty and over have the most discretionary income to spend. Yet, people over the age of fifty are often overlooked for sales and services. Without question, the mature market is one that—if properly tapped—can provide persistent and lucrative business for today's sales professionals.

Why sell to the mature market? For starters:

It's a large market that will continue to grow as we approach and enter the twenty-first century.

In the United States alone, senior citizens account for almost three-quarters of the nation's assets and almost half of its discretionary spending power.

The spending power of people over the age of fifty is five times greater than that of people under the age of thirty.

The Aging Population

Today's aging population is already having a tremendous impact on sales professionals. Because of the population's characteristics, the need for traditional products has been depressed, creating needs for new, nontraditional products.

Simply stated, the population is getting older, especially in North America. As recently as 1990, one North American in eight was over sixty-five years of age; in the twenty-first century, one in five will be sixty-five or older.

More than seventy million babies were born between 1946 and 1961. This is the famous baby boom that received so much attention. The oldest baby boomers are now in the middle of life and are beginning to think about their lifestyle after they retire.

In addition to the fact they are old and there are more of them than ever before in history, there is another fact about this huge population bulge that should be noted because it is of critical importance. These people are a whole new breed of senior citizens. If the human race has been successful in any pursuit, it has been in helping them to become old by eliminating disease and improving medical services. Yet, it has created a generation of old people who differ from the elderly of the past in three key ways:

They no longer fear dying young but look forward to twenty or so years of retirement. Once their kids have left the nest, older people will start spending their disposable income on themselves.

They are healthy and vibrant and do things that forty- and fifty-year-olds used to do. This is a development that was outside of most people's expectations as little as a generation ago.

Most are comfortable financially and many are very well-off. Seventy-five percent of households headed by someone over fifty own their own homes, and 83 percent of those homes are mortgage-free.

How to Sell to Them

Prospects who are age fifty and over provide a wealth of opportunities for today's sales professionals. Here are four important factors you need to be aware of when conducting business in the mature market:

1. The mature market is a cautious group. To sell to them, you have to win their trust and confidence. Sales professionals in this market realize that they don't have future years to repair mistakes or reinstill confidence. The best approach is a referral from a trusted friend or associate. The approach, though, is only the beginning. You must emphasize your professionalism and the stability of your company. Put simply, the over-fifty market wants the highest return for the lowest risk.

2. Use sales promotion material that includes illustrations and examples of older people (but that presents them as vital, healthy, and active). They will have trouble relating to brochures that depict young families and will be turned off by those that illustrate older people as weak and infirm.

3. Develop an approach that clearly speaks to their unique concerns, then test your approach on friends or associates who are over fifty to determine whether your approach is offensive or overstated.

4. Keep in mind that among their greatest concerns are maintaining their independence and their ability to contribute. Present them with scenarios that provide more than economic survival; highlight examples of community leaders, supportive parents, and so on.

A recent advertising agency study reveals that the over-fifty age group in the United States controls more than $130 billion in discretionary income—about 50 percent of the nation's total. The study segmented the mature market group into three groups:

1. *Master Consumers:* The largest and most important group, individuals in this group are fit, active, secure, fulfilled, and looking forward to their retirement as a time of reward. They are not seeking the fountain of youth. This group is described as "classic, not trendy, and never dowdy."

2. *Maintainers:* This group's members are financially comfortable, not as active as Master Consumers, and happy with the status quo.

3. *Simplifiers:* This group's members are older, less affluent, less active, and relatively light in consumer spending.

Prospecting Hints

In truth, the mature market balances its need for tangible products and services with an increased ability to afford them. Their children are grown or nearly so; their homes are paid for, or they have low mortgages; and their income level is substantial. In fact, the latest figures indicate that the median income of household heads in the forty-five-to-sixty-four age group is higher than the median income of all other households put together. And, although income begins to decline after age fifty-five, the fifty-five-to-sixty-four group's median income was still higher than that for all households.

Not only is the mature market relatively easy to approach and in a good financial position to purchase the products you sell, it offers additional advantages to sales professionals. For one, maturity usually carries with it a strong sense of responsibility, which results in a higher level of persistency. Also, older clients can be an excellent source of referrals because friends and family tend to respect their judgment and seek their advice.

Still, even though mature prospects may be receptive to an approach, there are certain characteristics to keep in mind when pursuing them. The one characteristic that stands out as a major issue with mature prospects is trust. Because of this, it's important to carefully establish a relationship based in trust.

Figure 5.1 is a sample preapproach letter that a successful MDRT associate uses when contacting a mature market prospect. This letter deals with selling financial planning, but it can be modified to address any products. The key is that you state clearly the need, why you can fulfill the need, and the desire to make an appointment.

Words from the Wise

Following are excerpts from presentations made by some of The Million Dollar Round Table's top sales professionals at its annual meetings.

Reaching Out

You can get anything you want in life if you help others get what they want—and this is especially true when reaching out to the mature market.

Sales professionals want to develop a profitable clientele among the financially mature. We know where the money is: people over the age of fifty-five account for 85 percent of the wealth in the United States alone and almost 50 percent of all discretionary income. However, despite its attractiveness and the progress being made by some, many sales professionals are ambivalent about practicing in this market. One reason is the reality that the mature market is not easy to penetrate. And there are several reasons:

> *The market is diverse.* Generally defined as people fifty and over, this age group contains roughly fifty million people (in the United States). With life expectancies approaching

Dear (prospect's name):

How much is enough for that "Golden Age" of retirement? Do you have a figure in mind? Do you have an age objective in mind, too? Maybe you've been thinking about a few years down the road, or perhaps you're planning to wait until the age when social security can kick in.

Those of us in the financial services business keep bringing up this matter of retirement planning because we're finding out some disturbing news—and we wouldn't be worth our salt if we didn't pass the word along.

As an eye-opener, recent studies indicate that almost 50 percent of all households are not putting money aside for retirement! Nor have they put any thought into how much they might need. That's disturbing, but it's also illogical.

After all, financial planning has done a fine job protecting homes and mortgages, children's education, automobiles, personal liability, and more. It has also provided income during periods of disability and helped pay hospital and medical expenses.

So why is it that 50 percent of today's households are ignoring insurance protection for their golden years? One thing we know for sure is that, on the average, everybody is living longer. It's been said that this is a "fourth-generation" generation—being a great-grandparent is no longer such a big deal. It follows, therefore, that in planning for your retirement years, those years have to be extended. Eighty is no longer "old." Also significant is the fact that an annual inflation rate of only 5 percent will cut retirement benefits by 40 percent in just ten years.

After all this, the question, "How much is enough?" has yet to be answered. Obviously, that's a personal matter, but it's one that I can resolve adequately to your best advantage if given the opportunity.

I'll be in touch soon to help you answer that question.

Sincerely,

(sales professional's name)

Figure 5.1 Preapproach Letter to a Mature Market Prospect.

age ninety, there may be a forty-year age difference in individual and societal life experiences in one market. So, when thinking of the mature market, think of millions of people at different stages and ages in life, each with his or her own desires and dreams. One size does *not* fit all in the mature market, and it is too diverse to wrap up in a neat little package, which makes it a market that requires focused thought and skill to penetrate.

The financially mature are increasingly skeptical of salespeople. Bad press about companies and sales professionals preying on the elderly has not helped. But even more troubling to upscale consumers is the lack of knowledge sales professionals have about the real concerns, interests, and lifestyles of older adults. This lack of knowledge is the primary obstacle to creating a satisfactory working relationship with the financially mature.

Resistance. Many mature individuals simply do not see themselves as older versions of their younger selves, but as ten to fifteen years younger than their actual age. With this in mind, it is no surprise to learn that many older adults resist such concepts as the inevitable decline in their health as they age.

But sales professionals should not be dismayed by the degree of difficulty in marketing to the financially mature. Who are the *financially mature?* They are men and women between the ages of fifty and eighty-five, having discretionary income and surplus assets. By definition, you'll know you're talking to financially mature prospects when those persons have more than enough income and assets to cover the bare necessities of life and are concerned about preserving income for themselves and preserving assets for their heirs. They want more out of life, and if they give you a chance, you can help them get it.

Another characteristic of this market is that it consists of two age groups: one from fifty to sixty-four (known as prime-lifers), the other sixty-five to eighty-five (known as seniors). Each has a different perspective on life. For example, prime-lifers may still be actively employed and earning wages. What is the percentage of wages lost at retirement? The loss is 100 percent.

So, while still actively employed in their preretirement years, prime-lifers retain a greater degree of control over their financial future than seniors because they can convert more of their talent and energy into earned income.

Autonomy

One of the deepest needs of most older people is for autonomy: the ability to make their own decisions for as long as possible. If it's hard to communicate with a visually or hearing impaired or confused older person, the professional's temptation is to talk only to the son or daughter ("What does your mother want? Does your father have any desire for the products I sell?") and to take the offspring's word for what the parent wants. That's where the need for compassion and patience comes in!

An important goal of any prospecting approach is to maintain the older person's dignity and autonomy as much as possible, and to carry out the older person's wishes as much as possible. Your job is to advise the prospect of the options.

Keep in mind two myths of old age:

Myth No. 1: Old age is a vale of tears, sadness, and gloom.

Fact: In reality, this is not so. Older people tend to be more satisfied with their lives than those of a middle or younger age. Of course, the above statement assumes that "old age" can be defined. And, after all, there are many individuals who are age sixty and over who do not feel "old." But for the sake of definition, let's assume that we're talking about the years after standard retirement.

And it's a fact that, for many, retirement is a satisfying and fulfilling time in life.

Myth No. 2: Learning capacity diminishes with age.

Fact: This is not true! The truth is that the ability to learn new material continues as one gets older. To stay mentally alert—to continue to exercise one's intellectual powers—will ensure a healthier, more satisfying retirement.

How to Better Communicate with Mature Market Prospects

"It is unwise to categorize people just by their age, but it is also true that certain physiological and psychological changes are associated with aging," says Charles D. Schewe, professor of marketing at the University of Massachusetts. "These changes affect a person's ability to receive a message. If your goal is to reach older people, you need to know how aging affects all facets of understanding."

Schewe says that older people have a harder time coordinating information that is hitting their eyes, ears, and other senses all at once. "This can cause real problems in communication," he notes.

As a sales professional selling products, you should be aware of these communication constraints. Schewe says the following seven guidelines help in any sales presentations directed toward mature prospects:

1. *Simplify your message.* As adults get older, their reaction time becomes slower and less accurate in response to sensory stimulation. "Because the central nervous system's capacity to process information is reduced, the elderly often miss messages if their attention is divided," Schewe says. *Advice:* Don't overload your sales presentation with unnecessary information. To borrow from a timeless principle of advertising: Keep it simple.

2. *Create familiarity with your message.* "Familiar experiences are easier for older people to process," Schewe says. "They find comfort and security in seeing and hearing events in the usual way." *Advice:* Try to personalize your presentations by incorporating your prospect's real-life experiences in your communication with him or her.

3. *Don't use abstract concepts when describing products.* "Older people rely more on concrete ideas than on abstract thinking. As people age, their problem-solving abilities typically decline," he says. Schewe notes that visual aids improve all recall for older adults. "As people age, visual memory declines more slowly than verbal memory. A combination of words and pictures is especially effective when targeting older people." *Advice:* Use simple illustrations that support your product information when prospecting in the mature market.

4. *Express the point of your message step-by-step.* "When designing a presentation for the elderly, space out each point you want to make," Schewe says. "Older people concentrate on the first part of the message longer than do younger people. If you present information too quickly, the earlier cues will overpower the points you make later." *Advice:* After each point is made, get a confirmation that the prospect fully understands the information. The general rule is: The slower, the better.

5. *Say it in print.* Deadlines and time limits create anxiety for everybody, but this is especially true for elderly people. "When older people are allowed to process information at their own rate, their learning abilities improve," Schewe says. He notes that written material lets consumers set their own pace; video and audio do not. *Advice:* Use handouts or "leave-behinds" after your initial contact with mature market prospects. Written materials that stimulate prospects to

feel a need about the products you sell will better your chances of conducting a follow-up sales presentation.

6. *Supply memory aids.* "Older adults don't organize or recall information as readily as younger adults," says Schewe. "But when you trigger their memories, the differences between young and old disappear." He reiterates that visual cues are especially effective. *Advice:* Ask your mature-aged prospects to describe scenarios where your products can help them or have helped someone they know. Then show them the best product that would fit their needs. Get them to visualize the product in action, and then reinforce the solutions it provides.

7. *Make good use of context.* "The more pleasant the memory, the more easily it can be traced," says Schewe. "Whenever possible, your presentation should stir recollections of pleasant events like graduations, weddings, and births. Any audience that feels personally involved will remember your message better." *Advice:* Talk about the positive things that your products can do for your prospects.

Yuppie Be, Yuppie Buy

Let's discuss selling to the yuppie generation—the traits and characteristics of yuppies, the various opportunities and challenges they face, the sales process, and responding to objections.

Research reveals yuppies are affluent but are also increasingly concerned with money management. Are you a yuppie? If you're between the ages of 35 and 54 and make $60,000 a year, chances are you might be categorized as a yuppie. The term, yuppie, emerged when young adults began trading in their Volkswagen buses for BMWs. Yuppie refers to young upwardly mobile professionals. Yuppies are generally people who have graduated from a four-year college, hold professional or managerial jobs, and have a family income of at least $60,000 per year. Researchers from Texas A&M University tried to determine what makes the yuppie tick. The name of the game for yuppies is the best—buying it, owning it, using it, eating it, wearing it, growing it, cooking it, and so on. Yuppies hire others to do things for them—from choosing a wardrobe to buying a house. They are into lifestyle and consumerism. They buy expensive cameras and sports cars and indulge in ice cream and chocolates. Yuppies live more luxuriously than the average American. They are interested in satisfying their personal needs regardless of price.

Several distinctive traits emerged from the survey: yuppies tend to crave status. They are self-confident and adventuresome, optimistic about their income, and strong in leadership traits. These success-oriented people are looked up to and aspire to be on the leading edge. Several marketing analysts believe that with the drive yuppies display, many will be called "boss" by the end of the century.

Today, yuppies face a variety of challenges. They must deal with money management, the stress created by a world of choice, trying to keep up with the Joneses, and the philosophy of aspiring to be superhuman. Yuppies have been blamed for everything from insider trading scandals, rising consumer debt, declining birth and saving rates, and the fitness craze, to the stock market crash and designer pizza.

An understanding of yuppie traits, values, problems, and opportunities will help you in the sales process. Yuppies are big on convenience and having options. It is important to make them feel that they are in control. Yuppies are very appearance conscious, so the dress-for-success principle certainly applies. In addition, they exercise and travel more, smoke less, and see twice as many movies as the average American. All these factors are important to keep in mind when meeting with a yuppie. Remember, you never get a second chance to create a first impression.

Because the yuppie thrives on efficiency, they welcome comprehensive insurance and financial planning. If they can, they will want to purchase a majority of the products to implement these plans from the same person.

Yuppies buy into goals and objectives. One professor put it this way: "If you sift through the yuppies' answers to open-ended questions in national polls or their comments in focus groups, certain things keep coming up: goals, focus, an agenda, priorities, a direction, a plan of action."

Yuppies tend to have small families, if any at all. Such families have discretionary income and, therefore, are people successful financial planners should be talking to. These couples can afford to aim for targets such as opening their own business or early retirement. However, such goals require hefty savings.

Dual income households have become the norm in North America. Today, close to 85 percent of married households have dual incomes, compared with only 39 percent of married households in 1961. This phenomenon is expected to become even more prevalent in the next century. What this will do to the quality of family life in North America is unknown, but it will most certainly increase the need for more products and services.

So how do you find these customers? The same way you find all of your clients—prospecting. Right. But how do you prospect to them? There are two keys: ask and qualify. Many sales professionals do not ask enough or do not ask consistently. What do you think would happen if you asked every prospect and client you saw for their help? Says one MDRT professional,

> In my practice, I often ask on the first interview because I may not get a second chance. Naturally, this depends on who the person is, the size of potential sale, and the general chemistry of the meeting. Rather than asking the standard question, Who do you know who just had a baby or just got married?; I expand it and ask, Who do you know who just had

a baby or just got married and is making $100,000 per year? Who do you know who owns a business that is very profitable? Who are the three most successful people you know? In other words, I qualify the question and, in turn, I receive a qualified prospect. In fact, we mention to our clients that our target market is composed of people who make at least $100,000 per year or have the potential to do so in the next 3 to 5 years. The most important task we have in our career is to find these people and get in front of them.

Another effective prospecting technique is networking. Through placing yourself in a variety of social settings, you can find out who the wealthy people are in a community. The next step is to find out as much as you can about them. Throughout this process, continuously search for someone you know well who could refer you to potential prospects in a very powerful way. Once they become clients, these prospects can refer you to others. For example, if you do a professional job for the president of a company, he or she will not hesitate to refer you to his or her key people. That is the ultimate power lead.

Another great networking source is the accounting and legal community. You can try to see one new accountant or lawyer a week. Says another MDRT professional,

My approach is very low key. I ask to meet them for 10 or 15 minutes or out to lunch to explain what I do. I suggest that in all probability we have or will have some mutual clients in the community so we should at least meet. Guess what? When I have asked, I have seldom been turned down. This is a non-threatening way to meet them and they look at it as an educational opportunity. Once we have met, and if we feel they are worthwhile keeping in contact, we ask them if they would like to be added to our mailing list. We try to send something to them once a quarter and follow up with a call or personal contact once or twice a year. It is starting to work for us and can work for you if only you make the effort and are willing to call. Therein lies the essence to the amount of success we have in our business. We can have all the sales techniques down to a science, be extremely knowledgeable and professional, but fail because we do not pick up the telephone enough. There are only two things we control in this business—prospecting and telephoning. I think we have made such a big issue of telephoning that it has become a real fear for a lot of us. It is just like everything else we do in life—it requires discipline and motivation.

Discipline can be learned, but motivation is an inside job. Denis Waitley, a sports psychologist, says that motivation comes from within. Managers can't motivate you. They can only encourage you. Either you learn to enjoy telephoning or realize that you have to do it to be successful in our business. Think back to when you were a child, or think of your own children. Johnny says, "I don't like to do this or that." The parents say, "You will never like every single thing you do in life. Johnny, you must learn that there are some things that you have to do even though you don't like to." Adults are only grown-up children. So let's go back to the basics, swallow your pride and fear of rejection and call the people. All they can do is say "No." If they say "No," you are only back where you started. If they say "Yes," you have the interview. Think of it as an investment. You invest $1,000 at the beginning of the month. You are guaranteed $1,000 back at the end of the month. No downside risk. However, your upside may be $2,000 or perhaps $100,000. Everyone would be lining up to purchase your product opportunity.

In many sales businesses, this opportunity starts with the telephone. You can't lose, you can only win. But to compete, you have to have the mental fortitude to take rejection. If you keep on trying, eventually you will win. You can't lose, you can only quit trying.

A huge market exists today in the form of the dual sale to married couples. As a rule of thumb, if the married couple is under age 30 or has a dual income, it is important to try to meet with both of them. If you talk only to one of the spouses, inevitably they have to go back and discuss it with their mate, who has not been a part of the process. Says another MDRT associate,

> Asking the spouse to be my salesperson, I am decreasing my chances for a sale, and the chances of a second sale or setting up a juvenile program are slim and none. In the case of the dual-income couple, there is an obvious dual need and usually, if both are earning an income, both have specific ideas about how they want to spend their money. If I see the couple, I also have the opportunity of prospecting two people instead of only one. I know this is not always possible. But I mention to the prospect that I have a family and therefore I can meet anywhere between 6 A.M. and 6 P.M. If they respect my family commitments and have any desire to see me, we can usually work out a time to meet with both husband and wife.

The most important element of the dual sales process is the needs analysis. Use a dual needs analysis in the interview and if they become clients, give them a finalized copy of their current situation. The key is making sure the suggestions presented are *their* objectives, not *yours*. The couple must buy into and own the buying decisions they make. Be sure to clarify your suggestions and give them every opportunity to change them. Don't be afraid to ask if they could get by on less.

"I often show my clients what products I have purchased and explain why," says one sales professional. "This not only explains what my products do but also demonstrates my own personal commitment to my career as well as the products I sell. Frequently, I've had people decide to duplicate my purchases, or at least adopt some versions of them.

"You should always give prospects hybrid product choices. They want to hear what's new and available. Usually, they choose what they can afford. If you are a client of our company, you will have lots of opportunities to say 'No' to new product pitches and concepts. A big part of the job is to help them make them feel their purchases are driven by their decision. If that is clarified and agreed to prior to closing, then it makes your client's decision a lot easier.

"Next is a plan of action. I approach this by saying that we want to be thorough but there is a fine line between thinking things through and procrastinating. Unfortunately, procrastination on these decisions can be disastrous. So we have to determine a reasonable time frame in the middle. In other words, when can we set up the next meeting? I always try to set up the second meeting, or what I hope will be the closing interview, at the end of the first meeting. If my prospects are bringing up other objections, they are usually asking for more information. Hopefully, I can draw out most of those in the first meeting. In fact, I need to do this to do my research and come up with alternate solutions for the next meeting.

"Just like everyone else, the yuppie will have objections. Although they should have discretionary income, many seem to think they don't. One source described the basic yuppie financial formula in this way, 'If there's enough to pay the mortgage, buy a health club membership, and take a winter or summer vacation, then life is good.' At some point though, a nagging worry works its way into this rosy scheme of things. The yuppies begin to wonder whether in 10 to 15 years they will be able to afford the lifestyle they envisage and want to build for themselves.

"I am sure you have heard prospects say they need to conserve their expenses and begin to plan and save at some later date. A good response is, 'Yes, you certainly can do that later, as long as you're prepared to live a reduced lifestyle in later years compared to your lifestyle today.' Retirees today seem willing to sell their homes and rent and live a downsized life if they have to. They have been through tough times before. Many yuppies haven't, and they probably won't want to give up their home or lifestyle. In fact, today you often hear people talking about buying a second home for retirement. In addition, the goal for many today is to be financially independent at age 55, compared to the traditional age 65. This kind of lifestyle decision requires massive savings programs."

It is beneficial to show prospects your own products and programs. Most yuppies feel more comfortable when they have a game plan in place for their future lifestyles. You must train yourself to think long term. Remember the adage, "Rome was not built in a day." Let clients know you are in it for the long term. Commitment and loyalty are forgotten words in sales these days. If you stick with a prospect and continue to be professional, he or she will eventually do business with you. Says another MDRT sales professional,

> I have been contacting one prospect ever since I have been in the business. I have either phoned him or talked to him in person once or twice a year for seven years. I think we will be doing some business in the next six months. It doesn't matter though. I know someday he will need and desire our services and products. When he does, he'll do business with us. I am building my inventory, filling my shelves with good quality prospects. When they are ready to come off the shelf, I will have a sale, as long as I make sure the dust doesn't build up in the meantime.

It is crucial that you diversify your sales practice. Specializing in the sale of one type of product or idea could be catastrophic. Yes, the yuppie is alive and well and here to stay. These middle-aged mobile professionals of the 1990s are self-confident and self-expressive individuals, affluent yet concerned with money management, and very influential in society. Yuppies are big on lifestyle and consumerism. They are committed to careers, often putting in 60 hours a week at the office, and frequently using leisure time as a vehicle for corporate advancement through networking. Yuppies are concerned with social status. They want the best and are willing to pay for it.

Yuppies view change as an opportunity and they value an overall game plan in arranging their personal lifestyles. You must grasp the opportunity to add these people to your client base.

The sales process with the yuppie is really no different than with other market niches. You must still work on the basics. The twenty-first century will be great for your business when yuppies form a large part of your clientele. An important part of your job will be to find these high-income earners through effective prospecting and networking and then call them. The key to prospecting is to ask all the time. Try to prospect in the first meeting if possible, and make sure you ask qualifying questions.

The sales interview should be the fun part of your business. Talking to people and helping them purchase your quality products and services is very rewarding. But remember, you do not get a second chance to create a first impression. The first 10 minutes of the initial interview are crucial. Try to meet with both husband and wife, especially if they are a dual-income household. Dual sales opportunities will continue to increase. Show them your own purchase as a model. Talk to them about their goals with regard to future lifestyle. If positioned properly, we will be there to assist them in these areas with our professional services and products.

You have probably heard the phrase, "The yuppie who dies with the most toys wins." The ultimate toy for the yuppie should be your product.

CONCLUSION

By now you know: unsuccessful efforts in continuous prospecting spell disaster to sales professionals seeking success in their careers. Prospecting is the lifeblood of a true sales professional. Nothing more, nothing less.

In the early days of America, there were two types of prospectors. One was the romantic figure—hard-living, hard-driving individualists who were out after a quick fortune, whose search was largely unorganized, without planning, and not too efficiently executed. They were for the gold nuggets, for easily convertible gold dust that could be panned out of the streams that flowed down from the hills. True, some of these individuals were temporarily successful, but in all too many cases, they would find a good haul and become rich overnight, only to dissipate their quick-found wealth in the saloons and gambling halls of the frontier. They were constantly either at the crest of the wave or in the deepest depression.

On the other hand, there were the prospectors who took a more farsighted view, who searched not only for the quick yield, but also for the lodes of precious metal that would yield a steady flow of wealth. They were the ones who planned in advance, who organized their efforts, who invested in machinery for development, who went about their work in an efficient and businesslike manner. They had no peaks or valleys but went after the steady production of results.

So it is with sales professionals today. Some function in spurts, hitting spectacular heights of sales and then easing up their prospecting efforts when they feel they are ahead of the game. True, some of them attain success, but they succeed in spite of bad prospecting habits.

Others, however, recognize the need for constant, planned prospecting. They plan their work month by month, week by week—indeed, hour by hour. Their high points may be less spectacular, but they have fewer slumps because they have a constant reserve of prospects and definite plans to call on them. And they are building for the financial security that all sales professionals seek.

With this book, you now have the tools for better prospecting. By borrowing from the wisdom of The Million Dollar Round Table's membership, you are on the road to success. And, as you progress, you'll develop more and more prestige in prospecting. And prestige is nothing more or less than what people think of you. With it, you'll widen your circle of acquaintances and friends, and you'll make sure that you are not only well known in your community or market, but favorably known. Your attitude, in turn, will reflect the prospecting habits you have developed. Ultimately, you will arrive at your desired destination—being a premier sales professional in your field of business. Go to it!

A FINAL NOTE

The books in this series are based on the experience of some of the top salespeople in the world. The secrets and techniques they provide will help you to prospect, close, and sell more effectively and efficiently, and improving these skills will improve your sales ratio and thus your career. You would not have purchased this book if you were not motivated by success, but does a greater volume of sales make you successful? All of the salespeople who contributed to this book would say that sales volume leads to success, but does not define it. In fact, all of the most successful salespeople in The Million Dollar Round Table are firm adherents to the association's Whole Person Philosophy, which maintains that to meet one's highest professional potential, one must strive to meet the highest potential in all other parts of life.

A whole person is committed to a life of significance, happiness and fulfillment and understands that leading such a life requires a continual process of growth. Success in any area of life, be it familial, health, educational, career, service, financial, or spiritual, is dependent upon success in and balance with the other areas since all areas of life are intertwined.

Sales is a career that demands extraordinary dedication. The hours are arduous, the reactions of prospects can be hostile or humiliating, and the financial rewards are variable. After a long day cold calling or meeting with uncooperative prospects, it can be difficult to spend time and energy on your family, on caring for your body, or on the pursuit of further education. It is not always easy to comprehend that good health, good family relationships, and a commitment to education will enhance your sales career, but the experience of thousands of MDRT members has proved this true. When you are confident, when you are healthy, when you live by a secure code of values, and when you are able to adapt to change, you will inspire the respect and trust of your prospects, and sales will follow.

From the very beginning, a successful salesperson must demonstrate responsibility. The high producing salesperson practices responsibility to prospects, in providing them with the best product to meet their needs and their budget. In addition, a successful salesperson must be responsible to herself, in putting forth the time and effort to do the prospecting that must be done to get appointments and to be successful. An expert salesperson is also responsible to his industry, educating himself and using good moral judgment to improve the public's preconceptions about salespeople, and responsible to his community, giving time, energy, and money back to the area that provides his clients and therefore his living.

For some, the responsibilities of sales are overwhelming to the point they are ignored, which is why many sales careers are so brief. For others, the responsibility of gathering and maintaining a client base can be so wearing that other areas of responsibility become subordinate. Persistence in sales can be as dangerous as giving up if the salesperson is focused on aspects of the career that won't lead to success. Often, the highest producers spend less time at work than those who are struggling even to obtain interviews. It is difficult to know when to draw the line between a persistent person and a workaholic, and, as one MDRT member points out, frequently the training for a sales career convinces new salespeople that workaholic is synonymous with success. As he says:

The [sales] business is a unique and curious business. We are attracted to this great business because of the opportunities and the unlimited possibilities. And truly, they are unlimited. I do not know of any other occupation where the average person, equipped with desire, motivation, and discipline, can achieve an elite standard of living and still be helping others. The successes of this business are paradoxical. The personal sacrifices and undaunted discipline needed to make it in this great business are also the traits that so often turn one into a workaholic.

In the [sales] business, we, our careers, our measures as human beings in the business world, are measured by the amount of money we are able to make. In fact, in this business, our ranking as individuals is based on the amount of production we do month in and month out—and on into years. Early in my career, I had been brainwashed in the same way, and consequently money and money-oriented goals became the number one priority in my life. Now I know, in order to become a truly happy and successful individual, and salesperson, one must write down one's goals, love and serve people, and work.

Isolating oneself as a workaholic will not increase sales in the long term. Instead, concentrating on changing one's perceptions about oneself, and developing and growing in all areas of life will permanently increase your ability to gain sales. For too long the sales profession has defined success in terms of monetary goals. The Whole Person Philosophy is designed to help you meet those goals while focusing on how to develop a successful life, not just a successful production year.

Career

A successful career is based upon four major components: discipline, vision, goals, and ethics. To become a great salesperson, one must concentrate on all four. To do this, as one MDRT producer insists, you must make a committed decision to be abnormal. Most people spend the majority of their lives striving to be normal—to fit comfortably within their community, their office, their group of friends. Why the sudden need to become different, to become other than what your peers are, to become abnormal? Because the normal people, the majority, are the status quo, who are mired in routine. To be a success, you need to be able to think outside the box, to question the routines and procedures that have always been followed "because they work," and alter them so they work even better. Unless you make a commitment to excel in your life and your business, you will be among the 80 percent who are normal, and normal is, at best, average, and, at worst, mediocre. To be a success you must be able to leave behind the comfort of rut and routine, and join the abnormal—the 20 percent minority of the population that is exploring and experimenting to create progress.

To leave the majority behind requires a tremendous amount of discipline. First, it requires the discipline to do what is difficult rather than what comes naturally: to analyze your actions and determine what works, rather than following the generally accepted procedure. Second, it requires the discipline to push outside your comfort zone in order to reach new levels of success when you are already successful. Third, it requires the discipline to realize no job is too small to be done to the best of your ability. In short, discipline is the difference between success and mediocrity. As a top producer in MDRT relates, "Successful people discipline themselves to do the things the less successful don't like to do." He continues:

> Successful people understand it isn't the big jobs which bring success. It's the little things we have to do every day. What will surprise you here is there are no extraordinary people, but some have disciplined themselves to achieve extraordinary

goals. Discipline not to go home on a Friday until the diary is
full for the following week. Discipline to break down the goals
into daily tasks. What do I have to do now, today, which if I repeat it day after day, will bring my goals to reality? It's what
we do each day that determines our failure or success. Success
is something we have to practice on a daily basis.

The discipline to become successful has to be rewarded by
something, or it would be simpler to continue doing things as you
have always done them. All discipline results from a vision. Those
salespeople who have the discipline to make success happen a little at a time derive that discipline from seeing themselves as successful. Most people want to improve their lives and careers, in
other words, most people want to be successful. In spite of this,
most people are unable to discipline themselves to think and act
differently, because they are unable to envision themselves as
successful. A respected member of MDRT explains the importance of vision this way:

> People of greatness don't get there by accident. The person
> who gets to the top of the mountain didn't fall there! They be-
> come masterful by making choices and decisions of exactly
> what it is they want to achieve. When you realize that the
> world we live in is entirely made up, then you are free to cre-
> ate the world you want. All of us know that goals sculpt and
> shape our lives. We know that, we've heard about their im-
> portance enough times haven't we? However, goals alone are
> not enough to turn your life into a masterpiece.
>
> Many people make the mistake of just setting goals with-
> out having something greater to live for, without a deep felt
> purpose at the core of your very being. As George Bernard
> Shaw wrote, "A purpose recognized by yourself is a mighty
> one." We need to go beyond goal setting, because goal setting
> on its own has limitations.
>
> Everything large is built up from small pieces; giant leaps
> are the accumulation of many smaller leaps. Realization of

your vision doesn't come usually in one move, but one step at a time. The whole is the sum total of its parts. What's important is that each smaller step is a part of the big picture, otherwise you can still be a goal achiever, and not be a success.

Think of your vision as a jigsaw puzzle. It can't be done in one move, or by rushing and jamming pieces into place. The only way is by visualizing the finished image and then working piece by piece, day by day. Then what happens is as you begin to solve it the quicker and easier you complete it. You build momentum. If you build a little on a little and do this often, soon it becomes big. Without a vision the goals will not take the shape of the whole, will they?

Your daily actions and activities should come not only from your goals, but from your vision. This will give your daily activities more meaning and purpose.

Your vision of yourself provides you the motivation to complete the daily tasks that are inherent in being a successful salesperson. Goals are the way you can measure progress in reaching your vision, and the way you can focus your discipline to directly lead from where you are to where you envision yourself. As one motivational expert at an MDRT meeting said, "goals manipulate process." Achievement of your vision is dependent upon practical application of the discipline your vision has instilled in you, and goals allow you to apply that discipline.

A goal is a piece of the jigsaw puzzle that composes your vision. With each goal you meet, you are getting closer to the success you envision yourself to be, and each goal you meet makes subsequent goals easier because of the confidence attaining goals lends you. For a goal to assist you in becoming your vision, it must be realistic. It is best to start with smaller goals, such as "I will call twenty new prospects every day next week," and build up to goals like "I will be my business' highest producer this year," or the system will backfire. By setting unrealistic goals you are procrastinating on reaching your vision, since each goal that you fail to meet will make you less likely to move forward. This is not to say your goals should be things you know you can do. As one well-known motivation researcher states, goals are most effective if they have a 50 percent chance of failure:

> What research has discovered, and what could be pure gold for anyone who understood how to apply it, is that your goals will continue to strengthen your motivation up to the fifty percent probability of success. In other words, your goals are most motivating, they tap into your most powerful inner resources, when you have a 50/50 chance at reaching them, when your probability of success is fifty percent. And no motivation is aroused when the goal is perceived as being either virtually certain, or virtually impossible to attain. This provides the answer for so many sales professionals who seem to lose their achievement drive. They have failed to use goals to fuel their internal fire, to motivate themselves properly.

Goals are motivation to maintain the discipline that is used to fuel the conversion of your vision into a reality. Every time you reach a goal you are propelled to achieve more, because you have the confidence of achievement and because you have a new habit for success. According to recent research, it takes 21 days to establish a new habit. When you raise the bar to reach a goal, and are doing something every day to ensure your success, after 21 days it becomes second nature—a part of your established routine. So, even after your goal has been met, you will be in the habit of doing something that has contributed to your success. Many people focus on the end, the meeting of a goal, as the main benefit, but the adoption of habits that allow you to reach the goal is every bit as important. As many MDRT members have pointed out, success is a process, not an event. The habits you develop in pursuit of a goal will make you more successful, as will the attitude you develop from the implementation of those habits. A top member and motivational expert said:

Ongoing action supports a goal. And whenever we are in action towards a goal, we feel better about ourselves, our energy is higher, our confidence and self-esteem are growing in strength. When we coast, when our achievement drive is low, our self-esteem goes down, we retreat into our comfort zones, and lose much of our enthusiasm for life. Our attitude goes sour.

Goals are important because they improve your habits and they alter your attitude. When we are efficient and we are full of energy we are more capable of success, and the more successful we are in reaching our goals, the easier it becomes for us to set more.

While determining visions, setting goals, and using discipline to reach them, one must be certain that the vision of success is based on solid ethical principles. Becoming a success takes a great deal of work and energy, and any path to success that does not include hard work and effort is bound to be faulty. As one member of MDRT says, "doing the right thing goes hand in hand with doing well. There are ways to become successful with no great investment of time and energy, but the success you will attain using these methods will be transparent and transitory." The only way to be successful is to inspire your prospects to believe in you, and this will only happen if they can see you creating successful habits and meeting goals. Instant success is possible through only the most unethical methods, that initially hurt others, but eventually will hurt the people who practice them.

Sales is a profession that is frequently accused of questionable ethics. We have all seen films or heard jokes that feature unscrupulous used car dealers, or salespeople who are thinly disguised con men. These negative stereotypes make it all the more important that your sales dealings be straightforward and honest ones. To find and keep customers you need to take personal responsibility for who you are and what you do. When your prospects see that you are someone focused on success and working hard to get there, they will feel comfortable giving you their business. When they see how your goal-oriented habits and discipline are put to work in their best interests, they will become clients, giving you more business, referring you to their friends, and contributing to your success.

This can be a slow process, and at times it will be tempting to place immediate success over honesty, integrity, and fairness. If you are to be successful in sales, you will be patient, and put in the hours and work rather than pursue personal gain through shady business dealings. A past president of MDRT told this story to emphasize how important ethics are to success:

> I think that sometimes nice guys may appear to finish last, but that's because they're running in a different race. For example, Australian golfer, Greg Norman, is one of the biggest draws on the pro tour. He was among the leaders of the 1996 Greater Hartford open, when he disqualified himself by reporting to tournament officials that he had inadvertently played with an improper ball for the first two rounds. That's ethics. There is no pillow as soft—or as comforting—as a clear conscience.

Questionable ethics may allow you to win sales in the short term, but long-term success is conditional upon loyal clients, who will only come to you when, like Norman, you admit your wrongs and prove your commitment to ethical business dealings.

To have a successful sales career you must be able to envision yourself as a success. Then, you must break your vision into smaller goals, and develop the habits and the discipline to meet them. You must live by a code of ethics that insists upon honesty, fairness, compassion, and hard work, and the sales will follow.

Education

Education is closely related to the area of sales success. Your vision of sales success can be broken down into goals, like completing professional training or designation programs, that will increase customer confidence and therefore sales, but education is an area of life distinct from either career or play.

As the inspiration for the Whole Person Philosophy, Dr. Mortimer J. Adler, explains, education is part of an important life category known as leisure. Leisure activities are activities that provide no extrinsic gain or compensation, but rather intrinsic rewards. These activities may be extremely grueling, but are worth doing despite the difficulty of the tasks. As we must have work in order to live, we must have leisure in order to live well. Dr. Adler explains:

> Leisure activities either produce a growth in the human person, a development of the self, or they produce advances in civilization, developments in the arts and sciences. Any form of learning, any form of creative work, any form of political or socially useful activity, is a leisure activity. Anything which contributes to the advancement of society is a leisure activity. It follows, then, that leisure activities are those which are morally obligatory.

As a sales professional you serve the public as a trusted advisor, and are responsible for being up to date with current knowledge and developments in your field in order to serve your clients in the best way possible.

Pursuit of education makes you more confident with prospects, and this, in turn, increases sales. Confidence is rarely achieved through public adulation. Instead, confidence usually comes from competence, which in turn comes from knowledge. When you increase your knowledge and confidence, you become more aware of your values, behave in a more creative manner, communicate things you believe in to others better, and are able to translate ideas into action through consistent hard work. Hard work without a sense of direction leads to frustration, but education can focus your work, increase your confidence, and help you analyze and improve your professional skills. As one MDRT member asserts, our success in becoming a professional human being depends very much on the efforts we make to understand and continue our own professional self-growth and development.

We no longer have the luxury of dying in the same world into which we were born. We are undergoing constant change. A development committee at Sony determined that at the current rate of technological change a new product becomes obsolete every 18 days. To be successful in an environment like this, you need to be able to think of a way to replace that product and get it out before the eighteenth day, so that you aren't surpassed by another company. Many people carry palm pilots. These computers, small enough to fit into a shirt pocket, contain more computer technology than was available in the whole world in 1985. The world we live in demands constant education to meet the demands of its constant change. A highly respected MDRT member sums this up well when he says:

> We need to continually educate and reeducate ourselves so that our knowledge and skills are cutting edge. As business guru Alvin Toffler says, "The illiterates of the future are not those who cannot read and write, but those who cannot learn, unlearn, and relearn."

Charles Darwin says the success of a species has little to do with its size or its strength, but everything to do with its ability to adapt to changing circumstances. The same can be said of the success of a salesperson. As one motivational expert says, "In a post-industrial economy, people aren't a factor of production, people are the competitive edge. If you're not educated, it's not that you will be unimportant to the society. If you are not educated, you will be irrelevant to the society. If you are not educated, you are not working." He goes on to say:

> In a post-industrial society, schools, corporate training programs, and seminars are the farms of the future. People are the new products. You are the new crops. We taught you to believe that education was the pursuit of knowledge. All you wanted was to make an "A" on a test, to graduate on time, or get credit for going to some seminar. But education is not about the pursuit of knowledge, it's about the pursuit of significance. It's about making a difference with your life. It's about adding value to your work and those around you. It is about giving all you can give and maximizing your talents. Knowledge is something you get along the way.

Education and knowledge are important because they change your dealings with other people, especially prospects, for the better, but they are essential because they force you to deal with yourself differently. Sales careers have a tendency to force people to see their success and significance purely in terms of monetary goals, which can become difficult to meet in this era of constant change. It is a comfort to pursue higher education in situations like this, because it relieves you of the pressure inherent in equating money with success. Education does not have to be formal in order to assist you in expanding your vision of success; in fact, one MDRT member feels the education he accomplishes on his own is as helpful as enrollment in any taught program. He advises:

> I memorize one message every month. Memorizing positive statements, poems and things, really helps round out, not only one's mind, but the way one views the world, and I need to start doing more of it. What we memorize is what we become, in part, a product of.

Education forces you to expand your thinking about success and about the world and your place in it. As long as you are learning, you are growing, and growth gives you the confidence and competence you need to be successful in a world of continual change. As a long-term MDRT member says:

> Growth is the only essence of life. It's a sign you are alive. Look around you in nature. Things are either growing or they're dying. There's no in between. In nature nothing retires. The masters know that there's no limit to their growth. The sky is absolutely not the limit! By continuously increasing their skills, they increase their abilities to add value to others. Change is a process, not a destination.

Education will keep your competence, and therefore your confidence, at the point it needs to be to help prospects through the constant change today's world thrusts upon us. It will help you to realize how broad the definition of success is, and keep you moving on your quest to become a successful person. The more education you pursue, the more you will achieve as a salesperson, as a member of your community, as a member of your family, and as a human being.

Health

Without good health, all of your efforts in improving your career and improving your mind will come to nothing. The biggest medical buzzword of the past two decades is stress. The complex juggling act modern life has become makes stress increasingly evident in all areas of life. For salespeople, stress can be especially detrimental. In a career with no set income, with long hours, and with daily duties that can be emotionally taxing, it is no wonder that many salespeople are not as attentive to their health as they should be. Although it seems overwhelming and discouraging at the end of a long day, most of the stress we are under is artificially constructed. As a stress expert who addressed MDRT says:

> Consider how far from normal stress your life has gotten. Normal stress goes like this—The sun is up! We need to kill a rabbit or pick some corn or something before that sun goes down. Come on, family, let's go do this together! So as a family you chase the rabbit or pick the corn, and in the process get some sunshine and exercise, roll in the clover, and take a dip in the farm pond. At the end of the day, you all go home and cook what you've caught or harvested, sit in front of the fire, spend time together, go to sleep, wake up the next day and do it again. That's normal stress.

The stress most of us deal with on a daily basis has nothing to do with this. We have plenty to eat, plenty to wear, and a warm spot to sleep, and in spite of this we work ourselves up about things that truly don't matter. For instance, did I call enough prospects today? Will I have enough appointments this week? Will I sell enough this quarter to take the holiday I want? This stress makes us unable to relax or rest, and lack of rest and relaxation increases our feelings of stress. Many of us use stress to excuse the things we are doing that are actually causing us more stress. Have you ever heard anyone say "Oh, I didn't get a chance to eat dinner last night, I was so busy working on that important policy," or "I know I should quit smoking, but I'm under too much stress for that right now?" The majority of Americans have unhealthy habits that contribute to our stressful lives, but we refuse to alter those habits because of a fear that change will create more stress. Thirty-three percent of Americans smoke. Ten percent of Americans drink too much alcohol. Sixty-seven percent of Americans are not physically active, and 88 percent of Americans have an unhealthy diet. And, if these physical statistics are not shocking enough, look at the financial and emotional consequences of stress. In 1997, an expert in stress told MDRT members:

The cost of this big life is formidable, for us as individuals in our business, and for us in our intimate relationships. As individuals, the incidence of stress-related illness has increased 800 percent, to the tune of $300 million a year in this country during the past decade. In our business the MERC Family Fund has found that, excluding retirees, over the past five years 28 percent of the American workforce has made voluntary changes that involved making less money, in order to feel that they can balance work and family. In spite of this, 40 to 60 percent of the people who got married yesterday for the first time will be divorced in seven years.

Stress is inevitable, but struggling is optional. If you want to minimize the negative effect of the struggle of stress, you have to take care of your body and maintain caring connections with your colleagues, your community, and an intimate loved one.

Although stress makes us feel there are not enough hours in the day, the only proven way to cure it is to take more time out of the day in order to care for yourself, your family, and your community. It seems like a paradox, but this problem can be resolved with minimal effort on your part. All that is required is a schedule that you will adhere to. No matter how complex your life is, everyone has seven 24-hour days to live in every week, which works out to 168 hours each week. Subtract from these 168 hours the amount of time you require working and sleeping, and you are left with an enormous bank of hours to do with as you like. Now, take this bank of hours, and subtract the amount of time each week it will take you to eat three meals a day and exercise three times a week, and you still have a large amount of time left to spend with your family, on your education, or for relaxation. Though these added commitments may seem to add more stress to your daily routine, they actually will decrease your anxiety if you adhere to them. This commitment to health will enable you to cope with the inescapable stresses of your daily life in a healthy and efficient manner, and introduce you to a method of dealing with stress used by most high-powered professionals; the Three C's of healthy stress. The Three-C method has three simple steps:

1. Viewing stressful situations as Challenges, not problems.

2. Commiting to facing the challenge.

3. Implementing a sense of Control over the coping process.

Acknowledging that your stress is artificial and unnecessary, and making a commitment to be as stress-free as possible through understanding that you are in control of the way your time is spent is a perfect example of using the Three-C method to live a healthier life. And when you are feeling good, chances are the little problems that can develop into stress will be solved before they escalate. You will find that by organizing your time you will accomplish more and be more respected in your career, your education, your community, and your family, and still have time to devote to your health.

Service

In the last speech he ever gave, legendary humanist and Nobel Peace Prize winner Albert Schweitzer said, "I don't know you, but I can tell you that those among you who will be happy are those who have sought and learned how to serve." You have learned that to be successful you must succeed in areas of your life other than your career. You must demonstrate a commitment to pursue education and a conscious attempt to be healthy and happy. Another quality that all successful sales professionals share is a moral obligation to serve their communities. The act of serving others enhances all of the other success habits. It will make you more successful in your career by introducing you to other volunteers who may become clients, and getting your name out in front of people so you receive more customers. It will make you more successful in your education, because you will learn how to apply the skills and ideas you are learning in classes to make life better for other people, and you will undoubtedly learn many important lessons from those you volunteer to help. It will make you more successful in your health because you always feel better about yourself when you are helping others, and it will make you more successful in your family because, through your example, you will be able to teach your children the value of serving others.

Salespeople owe a great debt to their communities, since the people who make up the community are the source of the salesperson's income. Despite this, it is easy to forget the importance of community obligations. As a renowned MDRT member says:

> There's more to life than selling. Almost everyone would like to exercise regularly, diet, and control their weight, to do things that will broaden their minds, to devote more time to continuing an intimate relationship with their spouse, to really get to know their children better on a one-to-one basis, to spend more time with their family, to be active in their religious center of choice, to tackle a worthwhile community problem, and to become more involved in our industry organizations. But many of us fall into a trap of feeling that the sales we make are so socially beneficial to everybody that we don't have time to get involved in any other aspect of our industry or, for that matter, in the other parts of life. But, the more we get involved in religious, community, and association activities the more we achieve a feeling of self-fulfillment.

As a salesperson you are helping people to improve their lives every day while you are at work but, as this MDRT member recognizes, this is not enough. To be truly balanced and successful, it is necessary to spend time giving back to your community in ways not directly related to your career.

Through volunteering, as a life-long volunteer who spoke to MDRT members says: "We find our allies. Our true friends come together to accomplish something. We find our faith, and we discover the power we have to change our lives and the lives of those around us. But finally, we find that to be a true hero is not to ride off into the sunset. The hero must always return to his people, to his community, to make a difference."

It is a very simple thing to volunteer to improve your community. There is an overwhelming number of tasks that must be completed for every community to be a healthy and happy one to live in and there are never enough people to complete these tasks. Churches, schools, hospitals, libraries, political groups, and children's athletic clubs are always in need of volunteers. If none of these places appeal to you, try your local paper to see if volunteers are needed, or contact an organization such as the National Association for Volunteer Administration (P.O. Box 32092, Richmond, VA 23294) to find out about various volunteer opportunities in your community. Some organizations that always need assistance are:

Democratic National
   Committee
430 S. Capital St. S.E.
Washington, DC 20003
202-863-8000
www.democrats.org

Republican National
   Committee
310 First St. S.E.
Washington, DC 20003
202-863-8500
www.rnc.org

National Parent Teacher
   Association
330 N. Wabash Ave.
Suite 2100
Chicago, IL 60611
800-307-4PTA
www.pta.org

International Red Cross
Public Inquiry Office
11th Floor
1621 N. Kent St.
Arlington, VA 22209
703-248-4222
www.redcross.org

Big Brothers/Big Sisters
   of America
230 N. 13th St.
Philadelphia, PA 19107
215-567-7000
www.bbbsa.org

Contacting the headquarters of these associations will give you information about volunteer opportunities in your area. If you are not already involved in your community, volunteer immediately. Success is sure to follow. As Ralph Waldo Emerson said, "To know that even one life has breathed better because you have lived, this is to have succeeded."

Family

The area in life where it is vital to be a success is with your family. As a respected MDRT member says, "There is no degree of success in the field that is worth failure at home." Your family, when you have a healthy relationship with them, are your greatest motivational force and support system. It is your responsibility to motivate and support them in return. To be a successful family member, you must place your family above the demands of all other people and organizations. Business, education, and play commitments are all secondary to strong relationships with your family members. If nothing else, you must make sure that your family eats at least one meal a day together, sharing and learning from one another. As one expert on family communication told MDRT:

> Other institutions have one by one stripped the family of its former functions. Educating children, giving religious training, supervising health care and providing training for a life's vocation were once the responsibility of families. Today these things are provided by institutions outside the home. The family has become essentially a group of people whose main purpose in being together is to provide mutual emotional gratification and shared joy.

In a time when all family members spend large portions of each day outside the home, it is essential that some communication take place within the home to provide each other with emotional gratification and joy. Since the traditional functions of the family have been taken on by other institutions, if your family is not providing this mutual gratification and joy, it has no reason to exist.

Making your family a supportive and loving group does not require immense amounts of effort, but it does require time. You need to be there to hear about your child's basketball game, or to help her ride a bicycle, or to help him with his homework, so that your child will be there when you need his love or her support. You need to be there to reassure your spouse when she returns home exhausted after a business trip, or when he has had a frustrating day at work, so that he will be supportive of you when you need emotional strength, and she will be patient with you when you are under stress at the office. The amount of time you spend with your family will provide you with the confidence that results from knowing you are loved, and thus with the motivation and energy necessary to improve the other areas of your life. As a well-known motivational speaker told MDRT members:

> My number one priority, every single day, my top-dog priority in life, the foundation for which everything is built is to make certain I get up on the right side of the bed. Period! It's my top priority. When I have a headache. When I'm fighting off the flu—it's to make certain I'm on. This makes me better with my children (and let me tell you we still have our differences, but I'm better). I'm better with my wife, and I'm more creative when I write, I'm better when I'm in front of people. It sets the stage for everything I do!

As this speaker proves through example, a thoughtful and genuine love of your family can be the impetus you need to transform your attitude and thus improve your career, and it is one of the most natural and simple things you can do. A high-producer in the MDRT says:

Being kind to others doesn't cost you any more breath than to blow out a candle. Wonderful things can happen when you say things like (to your wife) "I like your hair like that!" or (to your son) "thanks for helping me out that way, I really appreciate it." You are in a unique position to make people's feelings soar, and yours will soar higher because you learn that the source of all giving is love.

To be able to give love and support to your family, you need to learn to interact with them in a positive way. One of the best ways to demonstrate love for your family is through a sense of humor. As a well-known writer explained to MDRT, a sense of humor means more than telling jokes or laughing at them, it means maximizing the impact of all the good things that happen in your life, and minimizing the impact of the negative. Any time people are intimately connected there will be times they hurt one another, sometimes intentionally and sometimes just through carelessness. To have a healthy and loving relationship with your family, it is necessary to accept the positive and the negative aspects of an intimate relationship with all family members. It is also true that in the family, as in society, change is constant. You have only 18 years to enjoy sharing your home with your children. As one motivational speaker says, when considering your family relationships it is vital to remember that "today is a once in a lifetime opportunity, a kaleidoscope of people and feelings and events that are coming together just this way once and it will never, ever, happen again."

Remember the advice of a renowned MDRT member, that the caring connection is the definition of success. Men and women, work and family are not separate entities, but they are integrated. When you make the decision to put your family first—to make them your primary focus in your life—the rewards in other areas of your life will be breathtaking. You will feel more comfortable accepting career and business challenges, and your confidence and genuine love for your family will reassure prospects that you can empathize with them and understand the dreams they have for their families. The power of a loving family can propel you to do greater things than you ever imagined possible.

Whole Person Success

The concept of whole person success has been proven to work for some of the most incredible salespeople in the world. Every salesperson, in fact, every person, wants to improve—to better his sales, to better her life, to lead the highest quality life possible. So why is there such a large group of people who never change their routines to make success possible? Many people are unaware that to attain true success it is necessary to change your entire life, not just a particular aspect of it. Your success in sales is directly related to your vision of yourself—to your educational and professional competence, to your good health, to your pride in and aid of your community, and to your positive and loving relationship with your family. As salespeople you have a weighty responsibility to yourself and to your prospects. You have one of the most essential careers in the world. As a top MDRT member says:

> Nothing significant happens in this world until someone starts the process by selling. Nothing happens until someone cares enough to try to sell someone else a product, a service, or an idea. We are all salespeople. We are all selling all of the time. We're selling ideas, we're selling answers to problems, we're selling all the value you can add. We're selling our ability to manage and mobilize and motivate. We're all selling, all of the time. But, and this is important, not just anyone can be a sales success.

In order to be a success in sales, you must be a success in life. You must push yourself to develop into the vision you have of a successful human being. You must struggle to expand your mind, to appreciate and value your relationships with your family, to give your body the attention it needs to be healthy, to repay your community for the business and the sense of belonging it has bestowed on you. When you have accomplished this, professional success is sure to follow.

Beware the trap of achieving a little and becoming satisfied with that. As one eloquent member of MDRT says:

> There's one statement true of every person, which is that none of us has reached his or her full potential. Isn't this true? Wherever we are today, there is room for improvement. We can improve our relationship with loved ones. We can improve our business. We can improve our health and vitality. We can improve our relationship with God. We can get greater levels of fulfillment and peace of mind. We can contribute more value and more service to the world.

Success requires a commitment to constant self-evaluation and improvement. Your life as a successful salesperson begins with a commitment to becoming a whole person—to living a life of significance, happiness, and fulfillment. Commit yourself now to improving your education, your family relationships, your health and your community service. Your sales will improve, but more importantly, the world will be a brighter place because of your contributions to it.

ABOUT CFP

 Founded in 1927 by the most successful financial planners in the nation, The Million Dollar Round Table is now an international organization, with over twenty thousand members worldwide. The Round Table is an exclusive organization, accepting only those producers in the top six percent of the financial planning industry. An emphasis on the whole person, including family time, time management, education, professional behavior, and motivation is shared with members every year in the MDRT Annual Meeting. Members gather to learn from one another and from world-renowned experts in the industry, at times spending up to 10 percent of their annual income to attend, demonstrating the loyalty they have to the association and the value they place upon the knowledge made available to them at the meeting.

The Center for Productivity is the Round Table's publishing branch, developing information provided in the rich MDRT archives into quality motivational, educational, and training products that assist insurance and financial planning professionals in reaching the highest level of productivity. Established in 1996, CFP publishes in print, as well as producing material on audiotape, videotape, and CD-ROM. In the past three years, CFP has created products on a number of timely and useful topics, including technology, office management, training, self-study, long-term care, and now prospecting, closing, and sales techniques.

This book series, a co-publishing agreement with John Wiley & Sons, marks the first time information from the MDRT archives has been available to a general audience. For more information on The Million Dollar Round Table and the Center for Productivity, call 1-800-TRY-MDRT, or look through our web site at www.mdrtcfp.org.

INDEX